Adapting

to

Harmony

Life Manifestation to Soul Teaching

Ann Conover

Adapting to Harmony: Life Manifestation to Soul Teaching

Published by Wheatmark™
610 East Delano Street, Suite 104
Tucson, Arizona 85705 U.S.A.
www.wheatmark.com

International Standard Book Number: 978-1-58736-990-2
Library of Congress Control Number: 2007939228

Front Cover: Kirsten Conover, Age 9
Back Cover: Christopher Conover, Age 4

For Don

How to Use This Book

To best utilize this material, become familiar with the "Format for Healing" soon into your reading of the various subjects. This format is the template for searching out and bringing healing to core wounding, at human and soul levels. It brings together the primary touchstones—life manifestation, childhood wounding, and soul lesson—in finding the full spectrum of the meaning of our experience. Energy follows thought, so as you feel and understand the Truth, your heart opens and your energy comes into harmony.

After a while, you'll "know it in your bones" so you won't have to refer to the written format. You will ask yourself the deep questions as a matter of course as you walk through your life experience. The Format is not meant to be a rigid structure, but a guideline to be used with flexibility and compassion.

Look often to the "Processes," "Glossary," and "Notes" to be in touch with the clear meaning of what is being said.

Each subject is a point at which you can connect to your Higher Self and raise your vibration.

God Bless and Keep You as you seek and find the Harmony of God's Reality.

Much Love,
Ann

P.S. I have alternated genders and pronouns throughout the text, as felt most natural to me.

Contents

Introduction

We all have the longing to love deeply and be loved in return, to see and be seen, to find and be found; the longing for bliss without strife or pain.

Even though we've worked hard on our healing, humbled ourselves, tried to understand, surrendered, released our demons, and prayed, the same old problems keep turning up in the same old way. We struggle with depression, anger, intolerance, failed relationships, addictions, and fear. We still feel stuck. And, we are stuck. One of the reasons is that we keep missing the obvious.

In our search for happiness and peace, we don't notice that it's been there all the time, right in front of us. We're like the fish who, when asked about the water, says, "what water?"

We don't notice the harmony[1] because we're programmed to focus on what's giving us a problem. We aren't aware of our big toe unless it's hurting, and when it's hurting we make it the center of our existence. What's healthy and in harmony is the field in which we live, and it escapes our attention.

We're so conditioned to think of ourselves as our wounding, our defense against pain—so used to looking at that half-empty cup—that our lives become a see-saw polarity between closed-off, half-alive, self-critical thought/emotional patterns vs. ungrounded, illusory "happiness." We hold our virtues—essence qualities of God[2]—as valueless in the face of what's "wrong," or we defensively aggrandize our virtues out of unworthiness. We either obsess into or try to escape from what's "wrong." We push it away, run from it, and hide it from

---

1. See Glossary

2. When I refer to God/the Divine, it is not to an old man in the sky who metes out punishment and rewards, but to an omnipresent, comprehensive, loving consciousness that is an intelligent force, personified and not personified, personal and impersonal, that is everlasting and unbounded by time and space—and impossible to wrap the mind around.

ourselves. We are split and blind! What's needed is a "reality check."
We need to spend some time with our beauty and love for once. We
need a break from the illusion of fear, aloneness and lack and notice
what's right with us and with our lives. We need to come into balance.
We need a palpable taste of our true Divine nature, to discover that
we are a piece of God. Gratitude is the doorway.

There's so much about us that's pure and valiant. We Persevere in
the face of the vagaries of life; we insist on Loving even though we've
been hurt time and again; we Overcome obstacles; Hope rekindles
with each birth, marriage, sunrise, a child's smile, lover's kiss, and on
and on. We need to wake up to the Beauty in us, cherish it, nourish
it—"know" it in our cells. From this, we'll find the Beauty in life.
When we can find this place, life becomes astoundingly wonderful.
Things go well. Fulfillment comes in.

By connecting with the best in us, we connect to every one and
every thing. We begin to heal the deepest wound of mankind, separation from God.

From the "home base" of knowing our Divinity, we work our
healing process. The adult ego merges with the Higher Self and we
inhabit a Loving Witness to ourselves. From here, we can hold in
awareness the true context of our experience. We can see the problem
areas as a challenge, rather than a curse. We can step into the flame of
our fears and see them as our "growing edge," not allow them to poi-
son our lives. We can use our will to search out the Divine and bring
it through our personality, purifying what's unhealed. Through this
process, we create a strong and lighted bridge from the ego to higher
and higher levels of consciousness and experience.

The process of healing and purification is enhanced at this time
on planet Earth. We stood in line to be alive now! It's an incredible time of opportunity where the energies are high, both Light and
dark—actually, the dark is in its death throes. There's lots of support
from the spiritual realms, and from others in the body that are seeking high consciousness, to break the proverbial shell of our misconceptions and negativity and make an omelet. *Who* makes the omelet?
That's the part we've been missing.

At this time, we're experiencing a new paradigm of thought and
feeling, we're getting challenged to heal at the deepest levels, we're

learning about other dimensions, we're aware of a broad spectrum of life, and death. And yet, we continue to fail to adapt the life patterns of our negative conditioning to our expanded and deepened state.

At the soul level, we incarnated to heal misconceptions about the nature of the universe. We also carry the memory of the beauty, harmony and peace of the oneness. This is at once our healing and our reality, remembered and not remembered.

We find our way back to harmony through connecting to the part of us that remembers, healing the soul through the disharmonies of our life, and finding alignment—that is, all energies in service to the heart. A major key to finding alignment is bringing the mind into wisdom. This is where the logical mind merges with the heart. As long as the "conditioned" mind leads, we are like a leaf in the wind— we get pulled along in the wake of a split-off, mentally polarized perspective in the direction of the mass consciousness and our negative conditioning.

When we begin to master the conditioned mind through self-work and meditation[3], we use the mind to heal the mind, and thereby the emotions, and thereby the soul. As we reach a critical mass of healing, we find the mind that *wants* to love, along with the heart that *wants* peace.

Remember the prayer of St. Francis of Assisi:

Lord, make me an instrument of thy peace,
Where there is hatred, let me sow love;
Where there is injury, pardon,
Where there is doubt, faith,
Where there is despair, hope;
Where there is darkness, light,
And where there is sadness, joy.
O, Divine Master, grant that I may
Not so much seek to be consoled,
As to console;

---

3. See Processes, Working with Meditation

To be understood, as to understand;
To be loved, as to love;
For it is in giving that we receive,
It is in pardoning that we are pardoned;
And it is in dying that we are born
To eternal life. Amen

The Buddhists call this place *bodhichitta*, the mind of enlightenment. Enlightenment hits the mind, opens the heart and expresses through the healed ego.

This level of consciousness is something that we can claim as our own. It *is* indeed our own! It's the most real thing about us. It's a place that intends to bring peace to our own hearts by choosing to love ourselves as we are, and to bring loving consciousness to the unhealed parts of us. This consciousness brings peace to our relationships. It chooses to inhabit the "way" of choosing not to take offense and fight, but rather to hold the other in understanding and love. This is a level of consciousness that holds kindness as an aspiration, that respects and cherishes the self, and that aspires to respect and cherish the other. This attitude comes easily in some areas of our lives, and in others we have work to do.

Striving toward love is the way to happiness and, yes, bliss. It's the way to feeling comfortable in your skin, relaxing, knowing who you are, trusting and respecting yourself, and forgiving yourself. This is not a place of perfection, but rather a place where we have the knowledge that sometimes we are not kind, but the difference is that I *know* when I'm not, I make amends and continue to point my compass toward love. Why? Because I want to, I choose to, it feels right in me—no reasons are necessary.

This book is about making the shift in consciousness from smallness, limitation, negativity, fear, pride, and self-will to the discovery of what has always been there—that we are indeed love. It brings focus to using our free will consciously to choose the light in every moment, at every crisis and crossroad.

It's not a big shift that is necessary. It's only really a quarter-turn of our perception that's needed to shift our point of view and take in the fact that love, truth and beauty are the center from which we live and breathe, everything else is but a satellite.

This means shifting our point of focus from living in the blip on the screen of what is "wrong" and at the same time, becoming aware of everything that is in us—dark and light. We need to wake up to a knowledge of ourselves that transcends the superficial 3-D world. Jesus said, be in the world, but not of it.[4]

We need to step out of the pseudo-sophistication of the everyday world and wake up to the Reality of some basic Truths: The truth is that we are truly magnificent, loving, kind, beautiful, strong, and not only valuable but a necessary piece of the universe without which everything would crumble. The Truth is that we are Divine and intimately linked with every living being. The Truth is that every disharmony is present as a gift of teaching—we came in to experience those uncomfortable situations—and each is needed so that we can heal. The Truth is that most are unaware that they hurt you and it's not personal. The Truth is we are meant to love, forgive, give, open, and be hurt so we can continue the positive cycle of using the crisis or contraction as a signal to learn and open our hearts to love more. The Truth is we are a piece of God, and that piece of God is now and has ever been present in our own hearts. The Truth is that our love is the strongest, purest and most beautiful, the only real thing about us. The Truth is that the foundation of the universe is love. The Truth is that living the experience of Love is ecstatic.

Our soul work is to teach the part of us that is attached to the "safety" of contraction to adapt to the harmony that has been inside us all along.

"The fish in the water that is thirsty
needs serious professional counseling."

KABIR

---

4. John 17:14 (KJV)

Section 1: The Foundation

UNCLOAKING

The object of our evolvement is the uncloaking of what is within—that is, revealing our center[5], our essence, parts of which are covered over by the misconception of our pain, our defense, our darkness—the illusion of the power of contraction. Our "real self" shines through into our lives where we have harmonized with the truth of Love. Energetically, our light is eclipsed in certain areas by dense vibrational layers of fear—dark clouds. We know this by the manifestation of our lives. Some areas go well and others are always a problem.

Our essence—who/what we truly are—is energetic. It is a form that occupies the same space as our physical body, only in the next dimension. Its the part of us that travels from lifetime to lifetime, and moves out of the body while we sleep, perhaps to the schools of Shamballa, in the ethers over the Gobi Desert; or Mt. Meru in the ethers of the Andes Mountains of South America.

A deep and difficult part of this process of revelation is the exposure of the hidden "no" in all of us to God/Oneness/Life. To find it, we reach down into the depths of our psyche and emotional body to bring into the light our darkest inclinations. In making this energy conscious, we take responsibility for the "no" and, for our pleasure[6] in it. When this piece of anti-life gets revealed, it can be a shock to the image we have of ourselves, but it is a major step in our enlightenment.

To do this work, we need help to uncover the subtle emotional and mental currents that are the signposts to our healing. The Spiritual Law of Brotherhood[7] says that we should reveal ourselves to one

---

5. See Processes, "Finding Your Center" and Glossary (Soul, Loving Witness, Higher Self)
6. See Glossary, "Negative Pleasure"
7. See Spiritual Laws

another. It is balancing and cleansing to share our innermost thoughts and emotions with at least one other human being. It keeps us open, clear, balanced and connected.

Through this process we uncloak our Divinity, in this moment, in this life, in this skin.

> *"Any path of self-realization must deal with the most subtle, unconscious soul movements and attitudes because their effect is so much greater than most individuals only remotely sense."*[8]

DIVINE/HUMAN

The mass consciousness thinks of our existence as only our human body and our conscious mind. When we enter the realm of exploring the inner, these concepts can still be difficult to shake. In spiritual work often there is a split in people's minds that says either you are "of the earth" or you are "spiritual." The earth is generally considered less, even dirty. It's a part of us that we want to rise above.

This is dualistic thinking. Earth and spirit are one, each with its function and its place. If we ignore the areas where we are of the body, where we live in the world, and especially where we're contracted—that is, pockets of places where we have a "no" to oneness—then our spirituality is incomplete. As we travel the inner path, we slowly taste the pure spirit that temporarily inhabits the human shell. Although the body is a "rental," it's not in the highest to demean it or make it less in any way. Part of our task is to honor it and inhabit it fully—every cell—in order to fully connect with spirit. This is a paradox and a deep truth—the more we accept and enter the density of our humanity from our light, the more infused with spirit we become.

When seen and experienced through the eyes, ears, and feelings of love, the earth is a magnificent place inhabited by many kinds of beings, all on their way to oneness (or in their own realm of oneness—

---

8.   Pathwork Lecture #150, "Self Liking, Condition for Universal State of Bliss"

devas,[9] earth spirits, etc.). In Reality, the earth is abundant, beautiful, benign and healing. The healing energies of the oceans, rivers, mountains, trees, and flowers, all clean and clear our aura. The animals teach us many things, not the least of which is unconditional love. The energies of the devic world aid in the growth of everything on earth. They enhance every energy, animate and inanimate. The mineral kingdom gives us beauty and the power to hold and move energies. Our bodies give us the vehicle to affect matter, heal and find heaven on earth. These are precious gifts to be acknowledged, honored and worked with.

The primary focus of holding both the part of us that's earth and the part of us that's spirit is integration: the integration of child and adult; male and female; light and dark—the dualities. As we contain, that is hold with compassion, the parts of us that are in fear and bring our misconceptions back to their original Divine form, we heal the splits and build our light body. Energetically, we shift our overall vibration to a higher frequency. Emotionally, we transform our negative emotions back into mercy, kindness, gentleness, and love. Mentally, we bring the misconceptions about God, the universe, and life, back to Reality.[10] Experientially, we begin to experience in an integrated way (mind/emotions/spirit/body) the joy of the Truth and the loving foundation of the universe. We're *spiritualizing the material.* We're returning the dense energy of contraction (misconception/pain) into the fluid, harmonious movement of the state of oneness.

While it's necessary to hold both our divinity and humanity, we'll get confused if we try to mix levels. Often our humanity will seem to conflict with spirit. For example, when a loved one dies, the spiritual

---

9. "Builders…hold the form in coherent shape, transmuting, applying and circulating the pranic emanations" Alice A. Bailey, *Esoteric Healing, Volume IV, A Treatise on the Seven Rays* 10th Printing (New York: Lucis Publishing Company, 1980) p.421. "pranic …healing force…This prana is neither mental nor astral in nature. It is pure planetary substance or living essence, and is that substance of which the vital body of the planet is made… thought directed.," Bailey, Alice A., *Esoteric Healing, Volume IV, A Treatise on the Seven Rays* 10th Printing(New York: Lucis Publishing Company, 1980) p. 287.

10. See Glossary

part of us knows that we are an energy and consciousness that never dies. We may even have contact with that loved one after they have passed. And yet, the human part of us misses them. We miss talking to them, feeling them, seeing them. We feel conflicted if we try to dismiss our human "missing" with the spiritual truth that they've taken another form and still exist on another plane. We can't try to negate one level with another. We must hold both and let each have its space. Both realities are true for most of us at this stage in our development. When we all reach the next dimension, there won't be the split with the humanity—but there will be other work to do.

Another way we get confused mixing levels is knowing we create our lives and also dealing with the filters of our lower consciousness. I experienced a situation years ago while living at a spiritual community when a friend was ill. A member of the community called to find out the particulars of this person's illness. When he had the information, he said, "Well, I'm not going to go see him, because he chose it. He brought it on himself." Our higher awareness knows that the illness[11] was created by the person's higher self to learn a truth of the essence of God that has been forgotten. However, that doesn't mean that on the human level we close our hearts and say, "you created it, so you deal with it." We want to respect the human level of challenges and pain with compassion—knowing we're all in the same boat. We don't want to use a spiritual Truth in the service of our lower selves.

As we do our inner work and open to our spirituality, there's a growing awareness of the figure *and* the ground, that is, the self and the Divine. We're no longer focusing on only the figure and missing the ground. As we become aware of this figure/ground relationship, we can remember when we get caught up in limitation and smallness, that we're forgetting the context in which the self lives — the ground, the Divine. When we feel the pinch of that shoe that's too tight, we can bring ourselves back into balance.

Our spiritual connection is always infusing the harmonized ego with the experience of the harmony and the beauty…if we will only be quiet and listen. The harmonized ego (Godwoman) in turn uses this awareness to penetrate 3-D (what I can see, feel, and hear) conscious-

---

11. See Section 2, Health/Illness

ness and opens the flow of spirit through the levels; spirit through the ego and out to the world. This strong, living presence of the consciousness of love comes in through the crown, connects to the light in our hearts and moves out the hands. Here is the deep symbolism of the cross: light from the higher vibrations comes down the chakras above the crown into the body, through the center of the chakras and down into the earth, and from the heart out the hands and to the world.

As we practice this and make it a regular part of our lives to use our energy for love and service, the experience of our life changes. We begin to wake up to the present moment, which carries a sense of awe and delight. Life becomes infused with a new way of seeing that includes the immediacy of the loving God. Our body becomes lighter; each person becomes a loved one, the air smells sweeter; we want to play.

This experience of the Divine through the body, the senses, the mind, and the emotions has gone *unwitnessed* and *unnamed* in our lives.

You can describe this awareness of the loving Presence from different perspectives: You could call it a deeper level of mind that's more objective and not so reactive from the unresolved issues of our history. Or, to put it another way, you could say it's a connection to the mind and heart of God. In energetic terms, you could say that you're connecting to the vibratory level of flowing, benign, integrated energy. In emotional terms, you could say that you let go of your fears and hurts and allow the emergence of a joyful, loving heart.

When we're integrated/awakened/healed, spirit moves through our humanity.[12] The veil becomes the vehicle.

> *"My life is a prayer for peace.*
> *My life is a prayer for truth.*
> *In the apparent absence of love,*
> *I call for love unashamedly.*
> *For love is what I want,*
> *And love is what I need."*

> PAUL FERRINI

---

12. See Glossary

Transcendence/Transformation[13]

Transcendence is defined in the dictionary as "surpassing ordinary limits, extraordinary." In spiritual terms, we surpass ordinary limits by expanding into awareness of the bigger picture—getting bigger and bigger until we reach equanimity.

Through discovery of the deep, eternal essence of ourselves, we open the heart of compassion and bring the balm of love to the part of us that is contracted in pain. We transcend the limitation of our fear with the "extra-ordinary" view from the Loving Witness. Eventually, we transcend the mass consciousness, our limited concept of ourselves, the overly structured mind and our incongruent emotions and inhabit a state of being where the physical body and the ego become the container for the harmonized soul.

The dictionary definition of transformation is "a change in condition, nature, or character...change in form or appearance...change (an electric current) into one of higher or lower voltage." Spiritually speaking, transformation is bringing back to its divine state whatever in us has inverted into the negative, thus changing the energetic form from darkness and contraction into light. This builds our light body and raises our vibration into the stages of enlightenment.

The living of the dance from Transcendence to Transformation, and back again—in concert—first the right foot, then the left foot, then the right, creates the balance necessary for the walk to unity. The process is first the movement from our positive will toward opening our awareness of the Divine within, and from this foundation, initiating the process[14] of transforming the inversions back to harmony.

This dance becomes a self-sustaining positive vortex of energy—it propels itself onward and upward, producing more and more light and love. Each energy enhances and moves the other—first the right foot, then the left.

If we try for only transcendence, we may pray a lot, voice plati-

---

13. I first heard of the idea of connecting these two processes from the work of Susan Thesenga of the Seven Oaks Pathwork Center, Madison, VA 22727.

14. See Process of Healing

tudes, deny our darkness, and get trapped in the illusion of our minds into a false holiness. Until we can autonomously and consciously bring those parts of the self that hold against life into the light of God's Truth, we cannot truly be in the unified state.[15] The state of unity belies that anything is held back or split off from it—this cannot be.

So, as you set about doing the deep work of returning to the oneness, have a book about finding your light—your true self—on one side of your bed and a book about how to find your "no" on the other. Go back and forth, one to the other—transcendence/transformation—building the sacred space of and for your inner teacher in your heart and mind, while at once you look for the veils that hide the Truth from you. Sometime soon that which has caused us so much pain will become the means by which we expand into the ecstasy of peace and love.

Transcendence

The process of attaining the unified state requires transcending the limited view of our emotional reality[16] that we are separate and bad, and embracing our capacity for love and light, our beauty in the deepest sense. It requires the *will* that seeks to know our divinity, and know that it lives with our humanity in our own hearts. I mean the full-spectrum knowing of our mind, feelings, body and spirit. This is a knowing that we *experience*, and that becomes the state of our being, the state from which we live, and do, and be.

How do we do this in the practical sense? First, we make a commitment to our God and ourselves. We get to "know" ourselves as servants of love and oneness, and dedicate our life to the process of finding Truth.

On the 3-D (the world of the senses), we take the time for daily spiritual practice, reading high material, praying, connecting to a pure and egoless teacher—to enter and *continually deepen* the recognition of our divinity. This recognition is not a one-time thing. It is an *ever-*

---

15. See Glossary
16. Ibid

deepening certainty of our true nature, until this certainty fills every cell and every cavity of our consciousness.

Through our dedication to becoming more, we transcend fear, our emotional reactions, our judgments, and our negativity. We transcend the level of the "off"[17] energy with understanding and compassion for others and ourselves. We transcend the density of the materialism, violence and alienation of the 3-D. We live in the world but are not of it. In the last analysis, we transcend smallness. There comes in an expanded focus to the larger view that we have had many lifetimes and done and been everything—we are evolving, and have been evolving for a very long time, toward oneness—we are an integral part of the conscious universe. We become the creator of positive cycles. We are purifying all the time. We transcend every level of limitation and enter, bit by bit, the realm of complete love.

Transformation

Transformation is that process, which returns to its original form that which has been twisted away from harmony—reversed, inverted. Misconception comes back into the Truth, disharmony into harmony, the will to fight and negate into the will to love. Psychologically, transformation is the clarification of mistaken ideas into Truth; emotionally, transformation is the shift from painful experience into peace and joy; physically, transformation is the healing of disease and deep holding to harmony and movement; energetically, transformation is the release of stagnant energy into flow.

We transform low vibration from connection to our high vibration—the density of misconception transformed by the Loving Witness. You cannot transform something from its own level. You have to "get bigger." We know that we can't see from the vantage point of the loving force of the universe—God, so there will be things that we can never "figure out." We can, however, keep expanding our mind, emotions, and spirit, to find a level of awareness where we can witness and name what is happening. From there, we can reframe life from the myopic view of our wounding and defenses to compassion and love.

17.　Ibid & Format for Healing

We can get enough distance from our emotional charge to find the Divine Seed and our teaching.[18]

In order to transform in a healthy way, it is necessary to be well grounded in our spiritual practice—which supports identification with our Divine selves. If we aren't connected to the "knowledge" of our innate goodness, we will succumb to the belief inherent in darkness and contraction (present under the awareness of our conscious mind and in our emotions) that there is no goodness, no love, and we are totally bad. We have all had that experience where we have faced being wrong, and felt an all-pervading sense of ourselves as totally bad/worthless/separate.

In order to transform disharmonic energies, we must be willing to shift our focus from the outer to the inner. This takes consciousness and effort, for we are conditioned to blame the outside person or event or conditions for our inner plight. When this shift is taken, it is a major turning point and prepares our "soil" more and more deeply for shifts in energy and consciousness that is discordant and "stuck" into energy and consciousness that is in movement and harmony.

As we reach higher and higher vibratory levels, we continue to transform in an endless movement of becoming.

"The way of love is not
a subtle argument.

The door there is
devastation."

RUMI

DIVINITY/INVERSION

Once we understand and experience that disharmony is an inversion of a Divine energy, we see that the Truth inherent in this Reality is that harmony/the Divine is the *context* that holds our Reality. As

---

18. See Format for Healing

the realization deepens, we see that the Divine, that is Love, is the *primary* Reality.

While we may pay lip service to the concept that we are held in Love by the Creator, in truth most of us live our lives as though the context of our existence is the negative—we give our problems center stage. The shift out of this emotional reality, in general, happens gradually. Then, one day, we have an epiphany.

As we inhabit a strong healing stance from our Divinity, the increased perspective reveals that the Divine exists *within* the negative. For instance, judgment is discernment; jealousy is passion. If we look at judgment closely, we discover the presence of an ability to discern what is happening. If we take a close look at jealousy, we will see the presence of fiery passion. Where it "went wrong" is the judgment attaches a value of good or bad to what it discerns, and jealousy attaches possessiveness to the passion. So, an integral part of transforming consciousness is looking for the Divine seed in the negative.

The energy gets inverted by the misconception in the soul about the nature of the God force…a forgetting of the true nature of things. This misconception gets transferred onto our parents, and then onto life. This is the deepest layer of our problems with money, the forgetting that the universe is abundant. It is the deepest layer of our inability to commit, the forgetting that merging into oneness isn't annihilation. It is the deepest layer of our problems with worthiness, where we have forgotten that the only real worthiness—if there is such a thing—is the willingness to love. At the deepest level our fear of abandonment is the "forgetting" of omnipresence.

As we incarnate, the "forgetting" in the soul of the Truth that Reality is harmonic gets out pictured in our childhood. Here is where we can "feel" the pain of the misconception with God through our relationship with our parents—our parents being a stand-in for God. This must be worked on to understand and heal the emotions and the wrong beliefs in the soul.[19]

If we can be conscious of the Truth of our Reality, we can begin to shift our experience moment-to-moment, day-to-day. From the consciousness that Love is the field to which we are returning the dis-

---

19. See Format for Healing

harmonic "flecks" that appear from time to time, we can fully see that inversion plays the part of the medicine for the return to harmony. Intentionally seeking a loving state, encountering our blocks (inversion) and transforming them back to their original harmonic, is the circle of the healing of our souls

Before we can find the Divine in the other/life, we must find the Divine in ourselves. Our Divinity is the essence at the core of our being that for the most part we are blind to. This must be opened in us. We must bring our positive will to the task of exploring our deepest hearts to find, from a sincere place and not an egoic place, our beauty and our love. Its necessary to remind ourselves, and others, often of our Compassion, our ability to Forgive, our Longing to Give to the World, our capacity to Create, our gift for Healing, our Strength, our Passion, our Selflessness, our Magnificence, our Humility, our Vastness, our Depth, our deep Longing to Remember God in our mind, heart and body. When we see with the heart, we see these things.

In order to inhabit our full Divinity, it's necessary to reach a critical mass of *emotional* adulthood—that is, where we are identified with a grounded and strong adult that initiates transcendence and transformation of the "little ego."[20] This Godself (the adult aligned with the Divine) is needed in order to develop the facility of moving from one level of consciousness to another (child consciousness, lower self, higher self, adult consciousness, God consciousness, subpersonalities.)[21] When we can identify, even to a small degree, with the Godman/woman, this energy and consciousness provides a strong container for holding centeredness in the Loving Witness[22] to move through the pain and defenses of childhood, with compassion and understanding, to the spiritual issue with God/life. This deep witness initiates the correct use of our will—to seek the Divine—and calls for help from our teachers, both in and out of the body.

Each level is necessary. If we concentrate on the Divine at the expense of working through the emotions connected to our human wounding and defenses, we begin to inhabit a mentalized idea of

---

20. See Glossary
21. Ibid
22. Ibid

spirit. That is, we move into illusion. Not only that, but the emotional charges, negativity, negative intent, and lack of recognition of how we act these out in life, get covered over and ignored so that the wounding doesn't get healed and the darkness hides and gets stronger.

The seeking of our True Selves (the Divine) is a "training" into Divinity and bliss. It takes hard work, discipline, perseverance and a lot of courage. It also takes getting in touch with our heart's longing for love. Our deepest heart's longing is the will of God.

This process does not require that you withdraw from friends, family and a job at Microsoft. It is an inner thing. It is the choice to have the inspiration of your life be the embodiment of the state of being of non-harm, the awakening to the power that is in love, deep compassion for ourselves and others, the safety of the eternal and precious moment.

You don't have to *do* anything on the outside to be in service. You don't have to go to Africa to help those in need, although that is beautiful work. It's *more* than enough to bring "the compassionate presence" to everyone you meet. The presence of the Dalai Llama, even in a crowded auditorium, brings to each individual the compassion and grace of his being, and the high vibration of that energy gives to everyone. So, if it right for you to be working at Microsoft, it's ok. The healing presence lives in the monastery and it also lives in the office or the supermarket.

As we explore the vast territory of our inner selves, we find extraordinary levels of Divinity, and we also find deep levels of darkness.[23] We become familiar with the energy of an old word, evil. Evil does exist on this earth plane, although ultimately it is temporary and does not exist at the level of unity. It is, at the deepest level, in service to the light—through experiencing the inversion of the light in our misconceptions, we learn the truths of the universe.

I heard a Buddhist story some time ago about a great teacher who was instructing a student about the process of meditation.

23.　See Section 3, Forces of Light/Forces of Darkness

*He gave a long explanation, then turned his back, pulled down
his pants and showed the calluses on his backside. The teaching
being that you have to do the work!*

*"It is wishful thinking that concentrating on divinity and poten-
tial automatically deals with the dark side of human nature.
This cannot be so. You cannot overcome what you have not
consciously and fully experienced."[24]*

FALSE SELF/REAL SELF

We spend lots of energy in our lives proving that we're right and
ok, albeit unconsciously or semi-consciously. We do this because,
when we were children and did something wrong, our parents withdrew love and/or punished us. We learned very soon that our negativity brought dire results—results that felt to the child like death. As
time went on, we developed an idealized person that we wanted to
be in order to be loved. We kept giving this false identity more and
more energy and soon the fact that it was false got repressed into the
unconscious. Also unconsciously, we feel guilty for our deception and
this undermines our self-respect and self-confidence. Unfortunately,
the false self (mask) does not bring us what we want most, love and
acceptance—a sense of integrity and confidence, but pushes people
away and causes us unhappiness. We defend this picture of ourselves
"to the death." You know that terror that grips you when someone
insinuates that you are dishonest, incompetent, stupid, insensitive,
wrong!? We have to go looking in just these places to find this con-
struct that we've carefully made. We have to feel into the places where
we can't bear for people to see us in a certain way, and conversely,
where we *must* be seen as a certain way. We have to look beneath the
surface of our "reasons" to where our emotions, thoughts and actions
are not congruent. For example, when we give and don't feel like giving, where we act loving but we feel angry.

---

24. Pathwork Lecture #193, "Resume of the Basic Principles of the Pathwork:
Aim and Process"

As we are looking for the negative currents that are hiding behind the mask, it is necessary to remember that the bright light of our love[25] is under the mask and lower energies. Without awareness of the full picture, it would be impossible to do this work in a complete way.

The mask is present in certain areas of our life. In other areas, we live authentic, in our Real Self.

There is no quick fix or magic pill. When the negative in us shows up, we need to hold it in its positive light, as the medicine for our healing, in order to keep our energy moving—movement is life, stagnation is anti-life. Our child consciousness fears the lower self. Our mask denies its existence. And, the conscious mind rationalizes it away. Spiritual misconceptions believe that there is no love, and we are dark at the core. This is a difficult place to look in the eye, but we must align with our Godman and Godwoman and have the courage to face everything in us for deep transformation.

In the larger picture, we need the "negative" at this point in our evolution, so we can find our way. We can't know forgiveness if we haven't been hurt. We can't know strength if we haven't felt weakness. How would we know the difference?

> *"Through the gateway of feeling your weakness lies your strength.*
> *Through the gateway of feeling your pain lies your pleasure and joy,*
> *Through the gateway of feeling your fear lies your security and safety.*
> *Through the gateway of feeling your loneliness lies your capacity to have fulfillment, love and companionship.*
> *Through the gateway of your hopelessness lies true and justified hope.*
> *Through the gateway of accepting the lacks in your childhood lies your fulfillment now."[26]*

---

25. See Section 1, False Self/Real Self

26. Pathwork Lecture # 190, "Experiencing all Feelings, Including Fear—The Dynamics of Laziness"

EITHER-OR/AND-BOTH

The concept of either-or/and-both is really about the way we deeply hold life, our unconscious, or semi-conscious attitude. We are conditioned to think/feel in terms of either-or. It is either this or that. Whatever "it" is, it is either good or bad, white or black, mine or yours, right or wrong. As long as we live at this level of consciousness and try to hold onto either end of a polarity, we must be in pain.

Although life on planet earth looks at first glance as though there are only opposites, the harmony in life comes from holding the paradox. Mom is both good and bad. I am both good and bad. Both are true. Ultimately, there is no good and bad, there is only what is. No value judgment is required. There is no need to blame. There is only what I came here to learn, through you. You are my relationship with God in this moment.

An essential step toward unity is the intention to hold both—of anything. In one hand the negativity of mother, and in the other her love. In one hand holding our hatred, and in the other holding our love; in one hand our light and in the other our darkness. We are truly *both* beneath the surface, where another, more gentle, reality awaits.

Through reaching down below the level of our dualistic conditioning, we can find the wisdom and strength to hold the polarities[27] and the multiple facets of who we are. We have actually been living in at least two states of consciousness at once but haven't recognized it as such. When we're in the mask, we don't recognize our Godwoman that is good and compassionate. When we're in the "good space" we forget about the "other side." What's needed is to *open to the possibility* that we are *both*, and the *conscious* awareness of multiple levels will arise. Then we take a quantum leap. The character of our ground of being is deeply changed by this shift in consciousness, and we enter a more secure reality of self-honesty and the choice to align with our loving essence. This healthy alignment increases our identification with the Godwoman and creates the foundation to actively become our own teacher and wake up to our own wisdom.

Embodying the state of holding multiple levels of consciousness

---

27. See Glossary

will also help us to discern the Truth of situations where a negative energy gets attached to a positive energy. For instance, we may want to help a friend who is very appreciative, but we may also allow him/her to pull energy from us, depleting our life force. We allow this because of childhood wounding that says something like, "I'm supposed to give myself away." So, we are positively involved and negatively involved. We are only marginally aware that we are uncomfortable in the situation. From the mind, we may say to ourselves, "I don't understand why I resent her, she's in trouble now and really needs help." This is confusing when we have only a limited view.

As we enter the reality of "and/both" it becomes increasingly clear that darkness is illusion. It no longer stops us, and we use it to heal. The denser pole becomes less and less significant. It becomes a blip on the screen of beauty and peace.

> *"To love deeply in one direction makes us more loving in all others."*
>
> Fortune Cookie

Conscious Mind/Consciousness

Most of us think that our conscious mind is "us." In a way, this is true because we do become what we think. However, there is much, much more.

There are, actually, levels of the conscious mind, and then levels beyond that. To get a handle on what we're talking about, lets look at some levels of the mind. First, the instinctual mind. This is a thought/feel connected with basic survival of the body (1st chakra).[28] We're all familiar with the instinct of the body to live, the instinct to protect our children, etc. When this energy is clear, it guides us on fundamental physical levels.

Next, there is the child mind (2nd chakra). This is a thought/feel of beliefs about life that come from our parents. These beliefs are both wrong beliefs and harmonized beliefs. The harmonized beliefs be-

---

28. See Additional Materials, Chakra Consciousness

ing those that don't cause us pain, that is, they are aligned with love. Wrong beliefs are discordant, cause us pain and are misconceptions about the nature of life/love. There is also a kind of instinctual mind in the child consciousness that knows through the senses and can pick up energies of kindness, anger, etc. This thought/feel "knows" who to back away from and who to move closer to.

The next level of mind is the adult ego mind (3rd chakra). This level can "contain" the instinctual mind and child mind, but is limited in scope to time-space reality, the 3D (the seeing, hearing, touching world - illusion). This level of consciousness believes that what we think is who we are, what we feel is who we are, and rationalizes what we do. Furthermore, it believes that the thoughts we have are not only who we are, but that they are of value. (When you watch your thoughts, it becomes evident that, except for some volitional thoughts, most of them have utterly no value at all—they are "tapes" from the past and/or our conditioning, in fear of the future, and cling or fantasize).

This adult mind contains a conscience, a kind of admonishing self. The knowledge of this level is the intellect—things it has learned or studied and is limited to the 3-D world; the imagination is closely linked to the mental structures of society. This reality of the adult ego mind is largely limited to unconscious acting out from childhood wounding, defenses, and alignment with the "mass consciousness."[29]

Since it is based in a defensive posture, this adult mind stands guard against anything that threatens its "mindset." (The Buddhists say suffering is having a point of view!). For example, if you have a "love mask," you would defend against anyone who saw you as hurtful or insincere. The adult mind *believes* in the defenses of the child, and in limitation and contraction as safety. For example, we stiffen-up and contract our muscles if a car swipes ours. The adult mind has judgments about life, which cause suffering. These levels of consciousness are largely unconscious and/or rationalized.

From the healed adult mind we enter vast realms of consciousness (6th chakra—the inner/third eye). This level runs a spectrum from the

---

29. See Glossary

struggle to get bigger than our wounding to full realization of the worlds beyond the harmonization of the ego.

As acceptance is the portal to love in the heart, objectivity is the portal to clarity and purity of the mind. This is not only a concept to recognize, but also a spiritual practice. We need to find our mental center, our emotional center, and our spiritual center. Because we are so split, this process starts as separate practices, and comes together gradually into the integrated beingness of the wisdom, power and love of the heart (the Loving Witness—that is, the adult ego mind connected to spirit).

To begin this healing practice, we work on the mental body by finding a place in the deep mind, in the vicinity of the pituitary, that becomes a physical, mental, spiritual place of objectivity. That is, an objectivity born of a loving presence—not the heartless and rigid lower mind that will coldly assess a situation or a person, without considering the whole human being and without compassion.

So, we hold as our ideal and the highest Truth an objective place deep in our minds that can separate from our reactive (historical) emotions, and see clearly. This is a huge step in evolution. This is the opening of the "inner seeing" of the third eye. It's a place that intrinsically recognizes that we're not our emotions or our programming. It seeks out a higher "truth"—the Truth of God/Love.

Through awareness, meditation and inner work, we train the mind away from the "tapes" of our conditioning and the "automatic mind." A spiritual practice of occupying the "monkey mind" by using a mantra, praying, or chanting a name of God,[30] either verbally or quietly within brings the low vibration to a much higher level. By making this practice consistent, we bring ourselves into a constant state of prayer, and peace. After a while, when we "listen in" to ourselves, we find the old tapes have been replaced by the high vibration and the loving power of the "word."

The next phase is to bring the clarified mental field to the heart. This deepens the clarity of the mind in the waters of love in the deep heart. This place in the heart is not of the wounding of the heart—the pain and resentment and fear of getting hurt—but a place that is the

30. Ibid

vibration of compassion, the heart's wisdom (which is not a soppy, sentimental, wish-it-were-the-womb place, but a deeply strong, clear and pure view of life that holds others in good will and life situations as teachers). The wisdom of the deep heart knows us as being comprised of all energies—the spectrum of dark and light—and as, therefore, magnificent and wounded at the same time.

The deep heart consciousness becomes a Loving Witness to our process and is a state in which the mind is pure. From this Loving Wisdom, we become aware of the nature of true power—the synthesis of Love, Wisdom and Power. The Loving Witness carries discernment and understanding without judgment. The 'mind' of the witness has knowledge of the Divine through direct experience and knowing. It has grace, certitude and understanding of why we are here, as well as an increasing fullness of the realization of a beautiful and peaceful universe.

This inner mind is like our window, through which we can "see" the possibilities beyond time-space reality. On a practical level, through this window not only can we observe the limited thought processes of the 3-D experience, the emotional reactions from our history, the internal dialogues, and how we act out our defenses, but also we can make a healing *bridge* between the outer world and the inner deep knowing. It discriminates "who" is talking, among the myriad of energetic "voices" we have inside. It becomes the manager on the psychological level and our inner guide on the spiritual level. It has the ear to hear guidance. It discerns deep Truth and lovingly applies it to the places that are in pain. It becomes home base, intellectually, emotionally and spiritually. It is our center, finally a Reality we can trust.

The Loving Witness, this deeper level of mind, sees a different world than only the conscious mind. It includes the conscious mind, but infuses it with a wider range of awareness, equanimity, and compassion. There is a process of deepening that happens as our sense of identity shifts into a higher vibration—one that is more loving. This deep consciousness is compassionate, permeated with spirit, and *wants* to love.

Finding this place is a significant step in our evolution. It is bedrock. Interestingly, the real bedrock is not something we have been conditioned to trust. We've been conditioned to trust things that are inherently unstable, like our emotions and a level of mind that is "logical" but subject to wrong beliefs about the nature of life (from our childhood/soul).

The witness has a deeper perspective that helps us distinguish between our fears, pride and self-will, and God's will. This is the beginning of mastery of the earthly dimensions of the conscious mind—not mastery as the unharmonized ego would hold it, aggrandized and full of itself, but rather a being that has taken control of itself and it's path in a good way. This is a being who knows who it is, why it is here, and knows its magnificence and its faults—the places where you choose to love, and the place where you can still fall into the pit of your reactions and pain. It can identify, heal and leave behind, to a great extent, the reactive mind run by the wounded child. It can find the jewels in the swamp of illusion. It finds deep clarity and understanding because it is free of the confusion of our wounding, defenses and attachment to the outside world. The Loving Witness becomes more and more pure, and the mind increasingly perceives the loving universe. What was before a world filled with discontent and pain, becomes an earthly paradise.

"Go thy way; and as thou hast believed, so be it done unto thee."[31]

INTENTION/THE THING

We like to codify strict rules about what is good and what is bad. We're most comfortable with a simple, unassailable *rule*. The deeper truth, however, is it's never the thing we do or think or feel that is the determiner of the light or darkness of it.

The truth of "the thing" always comes from the intention that drives it. We try to find "the truth" in our own minds, and have probably argued it a few times. We all have a knowing that there is a cardinal rule here, but pinning it down is so elusive! Yes, there is a highest truth. We find it by going to our deepest witness.

We know, for instance, that the taking of a life can come from

---

31.   Matthew 8:13 (KJV)

vastly different intentions. It is not a static thing, and trying to make it static comes from our fear of taking responsibility. It is much "easier" to say, "this is the rule no matter what," than to listen to the circumstances and be willing to take a stand for what is right. If someone we love is in unbearable pain without hope of recovery and asks us to help them die, what is the loving thing to do? The only refusal would come from fear, with perhaps the "red herring" of "It's not right to take a life" as an excuse for, "I'm afraid to take this action." We euthanize a horse, or a dog or cat out of our compassion because somehow we devalue a "lower" life form, so it doesn't matter so much.

There is also the difference in thieves. If someone steals a loaf of bread to feed his family because they are starving, that is vastly different from stealing that same loaf for "fun," and is also different if someone is mentally ill and steals out of some misguided compulsion.

We must be awake, compassionate and courageous to bring deep wisdom and flexibility to each situation; to consider the full picture of what is occurring or has occurred and bring the heart, mind and will together to stand in the Truth.

We look at the outside, the superficial reality –"the thing"-- when we give someone a book about a subject *we're* interested in. We're focusing our attention on the "goodness" of getting them a wonderful book, and ignoring our intention to manipulate them into liking what we like, or believing what we believe. Or, "I'll be honest and tell my husband I've had an affair," when the real intention is to get absolved of guilt, even if it is devastating to the other. (I'm not saying here that it is right to be secretive about affairs while married, but rather to be honest and clean about your intentions).

The deepening of our alignment with our Real Self[32] that is infused with spirit will help us to look deeper at a situation and not be so fast to judge or go with the crowd. We'll be more aware of our own intentions, both light and dark, and hold the compassionate heart space.

---

32. See Glossary

"Magnetic fields draw us to Light; they move our limbs and
*   thoughts.*
But it is still dark; if our hearts do not hold a lantern,
We will stumble over each other,
Huddled beneath the sky
As we are."

RUMI

DEVOTION/CHILDISH NEED

Something that is so often missing in spiritual unfolding is opening to devotion. There is a place deep inside our hearts that longs
for the experience—the state of being—of deep, earnest affection
and love for God, for life, for someone. The place of which I speak
is a juicy place, an "alive" place. It is the unbridled expansion into the
Deep Love. This deep Love is pure and unconditional, and comes
from oneness through the human heart. It's the ecstasy of finding the
love of the creator within the human relationship—and more. It is the
human relationship that is an aspect, a doorway, into the ecstatic joy
of devotion to God. It is at once palpable and ephemeral. The spiritual
and human radical loving becomes synergistic—each giving the other
depth and strength.

Real and true devotion comes from a clear presence in the moment and an intensely alive relationship with the Divine—both
within and without. It is not prayers by rote, mindless platitudes, or
empty "I love you's."

This deep loving and devotion comes from a place inside us that is
autonomous on earthly and spiritual levels, and from which we walk
to God on our own two feet and bow our heads. So often we come to
God as children. The child needs to be taken care of, and cannot yet
walk the world and do their part in the community of man. The child
cries and reaches for the "parent" when they are hurt. They take from
the strength of the adult for their sustenance and protection. And this
is as it should be for a child. That is why, however, we are so easily
misled when we turn to God. God is the ultimate "parent" because
the force of love is more evolved, stronger and expanded in every

way than we are. It is easy to get caught in the child consciousness with this "ultimate authority." We transfer this "fear of God" onto our parents, and thereafter all authority figures in our life. Even if we are an authority figure ourselves by mass consciousness standards, making a big salary or famous, we still involuntarily cringe when we see those flashing lights behind our car—or we go into "fight" mode from rebellion, same energy, both child consciousness. So, when we pray from the child consciousness, we don't take responsibility for our part, that is, our piece of the disharmony. We see ourselves as the victim of negative outside influences, and we beg for God to step in and take away our pain and suffering. We vision in our mind/emotions (a think-feel) an old man in the sky, the "big" parent who decides who is going to suffer and who not, who is going to have lots of money and who is not. He punishes and he rewards, from a context outside our comprehension. He is a power to fear. From this place, we are begging children and we cannot approach God with love and from choice.

There are half-truths in the child's "picture." It is true that the "force of love" is all-powerful and awe inspiring, and we cannot comprehend its full Reality. We must, however become aware of our own Godliness, not from the ego, but from Truth. We must know ourselves, light and dark, and take responsibility for our energy—thoughts, words, emotions and deeds. We must open to our power and the fact that we are a creator being.

As a creator, we create every nuance of our reality. When we propel a negative energy outward, we have released something that has form and consciousness and that will come back to us. We may not be aware of the cause and effect because the boomerang may not return right away. But, it will come back, even if it's in the next lifetime. "We reap what we sow."[33]

We must understand that we humans have created the negativity in the world from our free will. And, although we are part of the Godforce, we are also a part of the evil on this level of existence. When we refine our perspective to this deeper understanding of how energy works, we can turn to the Godforce from our love, choice and responsibility and honor it from our deep heart that recognizes its

---

33. Galatians, 6:7 (KJV)

beauty and power. Then, we begin to fall in love. We are not always asking for things without paying the price or learning the lesson. We are, as the Godman, asking for help to love more, to be a better person, to align our will with God's will. We pray with heartfelt sincerity and full presence in the moment. These prayers are always answered, and from this place we can truly love.

When we take responsibility, it becomes less important if others love us—and, of course, they do. We connect into the vibration of the intention to love as a way of life so that what we send out comes back to us in a never-ending circle of the reality of the state of the loving universe. To our humanness, this place carries with it high vulnerability and bliss that rocks the foundation of our defenses. *We become the fool for God.* That is, a place that laughs at the ego's fear of looking foolish. It is a state of being that comes to God from a full heart and prostrates with awe at the profound Beauty of the Almighty. This is Devotion.

> *"I would love to kiss you.*
> *The price of kissing is your life.*
>
> *Now my loving is running toward my life shouting,*
> *What a bargain, let's buy it."*

RUMI

ESSENCE/FAULTS

We're conditioned to focus our attention on the negatives in our lives. We're not taught to hold the perspective of the whole person or the whole relationship when something goes wrong. We focus in on the "infraction" and forget the rest of our experience with the person, the group, etc. We also are not taught to stop and think of our part, or consider the right thing to do beyond our injured ego. We blow a ten-year friendship over one incident. We turn away emotionally—if not physically—from our partner over one thing said or done, and hold them hostage in our hearts forever after—continually building our case against them—bringing forth an attitude of belittling, or maligning,[34] making them bad and wrong and forgetting why we fell in love in the first place. We don't allow their good qualities into our consciousness. We think we know them because of this one thing they do, "I've got your number."

We focus on our own limitations, too. We're either beat ourselves up over our weakness, stupidity or transgressions (the tip of the iceberg of self-loathing), or we deny we have any faults.

These tendencies toward directing our energies into the negative, the hair out of place, are a bad habit that keeps us feeling miserable and destroys relationships.

Half the healing is becoming aware. If we stop paying attention to our "reasons" and just take a look at what we do with our attention, we will begin to stop taking ourselves to this hell. We'll be able to say, "oh, look, there I am again, feeling miserable about myself—about others." If we use our intention to make this observation from as objective and non-judgmental a place as possible, we can turn it around. We do that by first noticing what we're feeling. When we do this, we're already in the witness. Then, we need to give it it's right name—call a spade a spade—"I am steeped in hatred for myself," "I want to hurt him for hurting me," "I will cut her off for being wrong."

After we have found the truth of our problem,[35] we're able to come back now to a place of peace and understanding. We can look at the current situation in a new light. We know *why* we have a tendency to put our attention (energy) on the negative, reinforcing habitual patterns. Therefore, we can choose to bring in the discipline of spiritual practice and whenever we see that we are putting our energy and life force into a negative thought or emotion, we can consciously activate our connection to our hearts. We can say to ourselves, "ok, I have gotten a glimpse of where I can go with this situation and I'm not going there. I will detach from my anger, point of view, victim hood, whatever has been the old way, and I will look for the peace and the love." When you do this, your energy shifts into a higher vibration, your mind opens to another viewpoint, your emotional reactions melt away. You are connecting into the higher vibratory level of Real-

---

34. See Glossary

35. See Format for Healing

ity. This process pushes nothing down or away. It brings everything in for healing. It requires clarity, courage and perseverance. We do it a thousand times. After a while, it becomes second nature and we are in a positive vortex. As we rebalance our perspective, we can hold our faults with compassion and recognize they are the signposts pointing the way to the rediscovery of our Divinity.

We refine and deepen over time. Our energy and consciousness comes into alignment with the essence of things, our own essence and the essence of life. We can spend more time here now. We have learned to do aikido with the fault—take the momentum of it and move with it into our healing, that is, uncovering more of our essence. We can rest now in the safety and peace of our recognition of the true essence of things, and our place within it.

"Find that flame, that existence,
That Wonderful Man
Who can burn beneath the water
No other kind of light
Will cook the food
You
Need."

HAFIZ

Section 2: Becoming Aware

DRIVER/PASSENGER

We are conditioned to believe that we are a leaf in the wind—that life *does* it to us; life is hostile; we're helpless victims—somebody besides us is driving the bus, and that someone—or something—is malevolent. This belief is seldom articulated as such, but it's held in our unconsciousness attitudes.

So, we honker down and burrow into the hole of contraction and deep, inner immobility. We react to outside influences, which *make* us angry, sad, depressed, or happy. Under the surface of our busyness, masks, even our spiritual practice, we're not happy and think something is wrong, and it is. We're living in illusion. That illusion is disharmonic, and anything disharmonic is painful.

What's needed here is to look inside, under the surface experience, and find our emotional attitudes that are really running the show. We have to cut through all the pulls this way and that, and decide, among the myriad of voices inside us, to dedicate our energy and attention to our highest good. We want to go for the best in us and put our energy behind *that*. The pulls of our wounded child consciousness, our negativity, critic, judge, etc., need to be recognized as such, worked with[36] and relegated to their proper place, the passenger seat.

This decision is, of course, a process. We're the product of many years of giving energy to negative voices until their energetic form becomes very strong and a deep-seated habitual pattern. As we wake up to the power of our choices and move over into the driver's seat, we change our life. Its not an easy thing to stop a habitual pattern, but once we "get" how we've been letting a lunatic drive our bus, we can bring in strong intention to point our compass in the healing direction.

---

36. See Format for Healing

Psychologically, you could call the driver the manager. That is, the consciousness of our mature adult. Spiritually, you could call it the Higher Self. From this springs the Loving Witness.

The "manager" brings about integration of the split-off parts of the personality and alignment, all the while seeking connection with higher Truth. This place is not driven by the desires and imagined needs of the personality, and its able to *hold as secondary* the emotional reactions and wrong beliefs of our wounding, and doesn't allow negativity to be acted out. It can begin to embrace the energy that is "off"[37] with compassion. Thus, we begin to know the territory of what had been reactive chaos, and consciously take Divine control.

Finding the driver of the bus is a major step. It doesn't solve the problem of our difficulties, and it doesn't take away the emotions that are so charged from our past, but it gives us a little distance. That little bit of distance is gold. Now we can look at the briar patch of pain and conflicting emotions we're feeling and say, "Oh, this is uncomfortable. I stepped into that old familiar pit again. This is why I'm feeling pain, upset, anger, etc. Let me center in the Higher Self/witness/manager/ driver, and then I can take the healing stance with myself. I can be emotionally honest and decode those emotions." Then, I can track them back into the past, embrace the young part of me, satisfy her real need—to be loved, seen, cared for—not her false need—to separate, be superior, hurt back—and recognize my teaching here. Now I have initiated a positive cycle, I can step out of the old pattern and look at the web of illusion it created where I misinterpret what is coming to-ward me. Now I can look for God's Truth in the matter. For example, if we get angry and judgmental with someone because they hurt us, we know when we go to our "witness" (the bus driver) that, while the other person may be expressing negativity, our attention needs to go to *our* "emotional reaction" not what's wrong with *them*. When we are looking with a semblance of objectivity at our "emotional reaction," we can track its source to our wound—perhaps we feel hurt now be-cause back then, we weren't seen. We remember that same feeling from childhood, and recognize that our big reaction to the person

---

37. See Glossary

today is really that hurt from our history that is still fully present in us, as though the past were still happening.

Going deeper, we look for the wrong belief that came from that hurt. Perhaps it is, "I don't have a right to be." This is the deep misconception in our unconscious that has permeated our being and our every reaction to the world. This reaction has been an automatic one. There was no choice here, although we thought there was. When that emotion comes up, we immediately follow the well-worn path of our defense (habitual pattern) against the pain of childhood. Part of that defense is to focus on the outside, the other guy, so we never look inside at what is really going on—and, we ignore the wounded child within, leaving her in her pain to deal with the world. We, the adult, abandon her. There has been no driver to take control in a good way.

When we take the step to manage the personality, our healing process gets "reframed." It becomes beautifully understood. A laser focus brings us to God's Truth.

All the "he saids, she saids; the "I'm rights;" the "I'll show you's;" the "I'm bads—you're bads," et cetera, et cetera, blah, blah, blah's; all go away. We enter a consciousness that can witness ourselves living our lives, saying the words, thinking the thoughts, feeling the feelings, and recognize that we are not any of those things. We are a spirit of light.

When we can let go of our death-grip on the wrong beliefs and negativities of the personality, love arises. The love in my heart for you—that is what's important. And, when my Higher Self is driving the bus, I choose to go there because I realize there really is nothing else, nowhere else to go. I've been hurt before, and before, and before, and I will accept a Truth of this plane of existence…sometimes I get hurt. I'm not going to war because of it anymore. I choose to love you anyway, and to love myself anyway. When we let go of the dictates of the personality, there's a little voice in the unhealed ego that says I'm a fool, I'm being used, ridiculed, taken advantage of, stepped on…but I don't really care now. I'm sitting here in my love anyway, because that is what I choose. My true self, the eternal spirit, is driving *this* bus. As I do that, I come to feel and know a limitless safety and well-being—a connectedness and realness of myself that has eluded me up to now. I feel only gratitude that I am here in this moment, blessed in the most profound and glorious way. I choose radical love. It's time to leave behind childish ways, to transcend to the driver's seat, then beyond to the state of being in love with everyone and everything.

"Look what happens to the scale
when love holds it.
It stops working."

KABIR

BLAMING/BLISS

Where is the love?

This is the question we need to be asking ourselves. Not, whose fault is it? Or, more precisely the accusatory, "It's *your* fault."

We blame because we've been conditioned to do it. We do it because we have the emotional belief that it helps us to feel ok about ourselves, albeit briefly. If somebody else is at fault, we can rationalize that we're perfect, so we'll be loved. We try to maintain the illusion that we're perfect because we need so desperately to be accepted. Even a hint that we could be wrong, bad—flawed—is an enormous threat to our made-up idea of ourselves, our mask.[38] It can feel like our "life" depends on maintaining the illusion that we're blameless. (Or we may hold it's polar opposite—"I'm a mess, a failure—and its *all* my fault—that way we don't have to face the truth of our inner teaching either).

When we find ourselves affected—charged, our buttons pushed— we are immediately catapulted into a painful situation from the past—that's what those "buttons" mean. Triggered by an energy in the present that causes our eyes to scale over, we get lost in a cloud of unreality. We see only shadows of another time—malice, deceit, coldness, punishment, disrespect, rejection, and undoing. This unreality plugs our ears, so we hear only echoes from the past—we select parts of what is said to fit the old picture. The echo of the past is seen, heard and felt, like a stage-set that comes down and sits in place in our mind

---

38. See Glossary

and emotional body. We're back there again as though not a moment had passed between then and now.

Before we understand what is happening to us, we immediately go into our defense: reason (Wisdom essence), will (Power essence) or emotion (Love essence).[39] The reaction into our defense is automatic. We are not at choice here. We tighten up—mentally, emotionally and physically—and use this coping mechanism to be "safe."

It's a huge step just to recognize what happened in our childhood and how we reacted to it.[40] After we've let the knowing seep into our bones, we need to muster up our courage and strength and put a branch in the spokes of the racing wheel of our automatic reactions. It takes an act of positive will to see what is happening and say, "wait a minute, I'm in illusion here. I'm not going to blame. I'm not going to follow the line of least resistance (my defense)."

What are required to hold this level of consciousness are lots of courage, perseverance and sincerity. We have to realize that our defense is aggressive, no matter what outward form it takes, and amounts to packing a sword and automatically whipping it out whenever an energy comes toward us that "reminds" us of the pain of the past. Then, the hardest part, we need to be willing to put the sword down. In order to do this, we have to turn our awareness inward. We have to recognize that we create our lives and that others are merely players on our stage. It's really not important what transgressions they make. It's only important to the extent that we can become conscious to our reactions and let go of the blaming cycle. Our emotions belong to us; no one else puts them there. Others are only being themselves. They aren't consciously trying to make us miserable. They're doing the best they can. And, most importantly, they're giving us the gift of being our catalyst for healing—they are our "sacred trigger."

When we are willing to let go of what "the other" is doing, we are deeply on our path to purification. We have shifted our focus, come into reality, and are willing to take responsibility for our energy. When this happens, we can see what is the root of the problem…"Oh, this happened because I need to heal my anger at my father for leaving

---

39. See Section 2, Offense/Defense
40. See Format for Healing

me." "I reacted that way to my husband because I believe, from my history, that the man will always leave me." When I see my present situation through this lens, everything is distorted. I misinterpret actions and words. And, through this, I *create what I fear the most*—the man leaving me.

When I am getting clear, I don't have to jump to the negative conclusion that every fiber of my being wants to go to—the other guy is at fault. I can come in for myself from the strength of my heart and wisdom and say, "No, I'm not taking the hand of my compulsion, I'm taking the hand of my love for myself—I'm going to trust myself to handle whatever comes up. I'm willing to go out on a limb and love the man." I'm healing my soul here, as well as my wounded emotions and mental misconceptions. Spiritually, I'm remembering, through the gift of relationship, that God never abandons me.

We get our human/spiritual lessons by shifting from our habitual patterns and turning away from blaming the other, circumstances, and life; by being willing to let go, and open to the real heart of the matter—where is the love?

Spirit *will* answer. And, when we are sincerely ready to let go of our "case" (against the other, life, God), our hearts spontaneously open, and in rushes a tide of joy. Not only are we joyful and free, but we also see the Reality of the situation—blaming anything or anyone outside ourselves is a dead-end negative. Now, we can be more kind. We can live the golden rule.[41] The way we treat others is a measure of our evolvement toward Oneness.

> *"Out beyond ideas of wrongdoing and rightdoing*
> *there is a field. I'll meet you there.*
>
> *When the soul lies down in that grass,*
> *the world is too full to talk about.*
>
> *Ideas, language, even the phrase* <u>each other,</u>
> *doesn't make any sense."*

RUMI

---

41. Matthew 7:12 (KJV)

THE ALIVE HUMAN BEING/THE ROBOT

Most of us live from emotion to emotion, thought to thought, situation to situation, reacting blindly from our programming. We believe we are actively choosing our words, actions and thoughts. When someone insults us, we insult back. When someone hurts us, we hurt back. If someone disagrees with us, we launch into a campaign to convince them how wrong they are. If our bodies develop a disease, we "nuke" it with synthesized drugs. If we're depressed, we take a happy pill. We do all these things because that's what everybody does. That's what our parents did, our schoolmates, our friends—that's what's on TV. We live as though life is our opponent so we react, react, react from our conditioning.

We are also programmed from the past. We reacted to hurts in our childhood with protective defenses to cope, to stay alive, to be loved. So, here we are walking through our life not really present to the moment or considering what we are going to do with that moment. Our reactions are unconscious and automatic. We're robots.

Sometimes, often, it takes a crisis for us to stop and say, "Wait a minute, why are bad things happening to me?" "What's going on?"

If we follow this "unrest" (an itch to change?) we may read a book or go to a lecture and we open the door a crack to our unconscious motives and deeper purpose. We step back a little bit in our own minds and check out what we're doing. As we begin to explore our reactions and the "why" of the state of our being, we discover we're *not* at choice, our beliefs and convictions are not wholly ours, our problems are not the fault of others but rather our own creation, as are the circumstances of our life. Then we "connect the dots" of cause and effect, we begin to gain a different perspective. Another level of our brain gets engaged, a deeper perspective, which is more self-aware. We begin to recognize certain "proscribed" responses that come from our past—which cause trouble because they are separative and lead us away, rather than toward what we want.

It takes a big helping of courage to relinquish our "tried and true" ideas and places where we get a sense of stability from "knowing" we are right. And yet, it's necessary to have destabilization to unseat the old patterns that come from our wounding and defenses. We have to be ready to tolerate the unsettling experience. From it, comes more fluidity in our thinking, emotions, and in our energy (if you can see and/or feel energy in your body). And, anything that moves feels good and is in life. Life is movement, not the urging and compulsion of stressful striving, but movement that carries with it a quietness inside, a sense of lightness and rightness, of deep, eternal goodwill and the knowledge of the "stability of change."

So, as we discover our aliveness, we can begin to observe those robotic reactions. Then, we can take the next step and engage this deeper awareness to "help" the part that is on automatic from the past, and "catch" the part that accepts without question what everyone else is doing/thinking/eating/wearing/saying—and, what we've always done. We may do it at first "on shaky knees,"[42] but as we stick with it, we get stronger.

The part of us that walks into a real experience of the alive human being, becomes aware of the light inside that loves strongly, that wants harmony, that feels an impetus for giving, for understanding, for looking through the negativity we see and experience in people in the world, and finds our compassion. This "Light of Truth" sees the connection of all things, and can feel the camaraderie of those of us that are dedicated to expansion.

This "alive" human being cannot help but see the beauty and feel the gratitude in every moment, even in the challenges—especially in the challenges.

> *"There is a beautiful creature living*
> *in a hole you have*
> *dug…"*

HAFIZ

HURT/SAFETY

The Buddha said that pain is a part of this life. In the west, we not only don't accept this truth, but we believe if pain is present there's

---

42. An expression coined by a colleague, Peg Humphrey, California Pathwork.

something drastically wrong. This attitude leads us to resist it (which makes it stronger) and be thoroughly unhappy with ourselves and with life when it's there.

We tend to hold onto our hurts. Often, we make them a tragedy and blame "the other." We're constantly trying to find safety from it. We withdraw, we try to control others, we aggress, we submit, we armor our heart. We live half closed-down because we're afraid of getting hurt.

We use our hurts to hurt others. When we do this, we feel totally justified and never look clearly at *what we are doing with our energy*— energetically throwing fireballs, stabbing in the back, slapping; psychologically and emotionally punishing, undermining, undoing. We live in a hazy awareness of think/feel in which we feel pain and strike out. Although we're not fully aware that we're acting out negatively, the fact is that we are. We know it unconsciously and feel guilt for hurting others, or ourselves. Because of this unconscious guilt, we have an underlying disrespect for ourselves that moves into self-hate. We carry the self-hate because we know that on some level we're turning to the dark and allowing negative energies to work through us.

Through the back and forth of "you get me, I'll get you" we stay in the realms of darkness and keep postponing our deep healing. We keep choosing to act out negative energy in thought, word and deed, not realizing that we *are* choosing it. We cycle in it—all in the name of "safety" and "justice." Our pseudo-protection doesn't really work, though. We get hurt anyway.

Sometimes, we experience hurt when there is really no ill intent on the part of the other. We are so attuned to looking for it that we paste it onto the situation.

We are actually hurt over and over again because we haven't healed our history. Our wounding and defenses keep *creating the same negative situations and drawing the same kind of people.* The energies produced by our misconceptions have a specific vibration and *draw like energies* from the outside. We aren't aware of what is happening, and we can't make the connections.

What the wounded child needs is not the coping mechanisms of our defenses; but understanding and love from the good parent, the Godwoman. This adult/God consciousness needs to let the child know that he/she will protect against those hurts from outside by coming present and standing in front of the child to handle the situation, just as a parent in the flesh will put their energy and body between their child and a threat. Otherwise, the child takes the hit—over and over again, and the part of us that identifies with the child consciousness keeps getting re-wounded, and never feels safe.

As we increase our understanding of what is *actually* happening, and we begin to heal,[43] we can turn our attention to the antidote for being in pain—giving. Instead of nursing our hurts, punishing others, feeding our negative attitude toward the world, or pushing it down and pretending it didn't happen; we can let the energy move through us, heal the child (emotions), get the teaching and give from our gratitude.

The Buddha was right, there is pain. This is such a simple statement, and we would all agree. However, part of "listening deeply" to this teaching is recognizing that we must, emotionally as well as intellectually, *accept* this reality—it's like gravity, it's there and we can't change it. When we fight against it, we cause more pain.

It is also not an injustice if we get hurt. If we can tune in to the bigger picture and recognize that we create our lives, we can unhook from the negative cycle of "you hurt me, I'll hurt you." We can see the hurt as the teaching it is. We experience hurt because we are wounded. What's necessary is to look inside and ask, "What in me is hurt by this, how does this situation connect to my history? What is my part in the situation? How much distance is there for me to go inside from what I'm feeling now to compassion for the person that triggered the hurt in me?" Whatever that distance is, it represents the level of *my* wounding, *my* misconception. If we don't have a "receptor site"[44] for a negative energy, it can't land.

Our unhealed emotions are actually reacting to something that is not personal out there in the other. Their negativity is actually toward their mother or father; and at the deepest level, God. It's none of your business, except to draw a boundary and/or say "ouch" in some way. We have to give each other a little room for our unhealed places. And, in the long run, we have to trust Divine justice.

---

43. See Format for Healing
44. See Glossary

So, as we reframe our experience, it's necessary to turn to another way of responding to our pain besides going into contraction and holding onto it. When we can relax into this reality that is life on planet earth, we can learn to allow ourselves to feel fully the pain of the arrow in our heart ("Oh, that arrow in my heart hurts like hell"), name the energy and without pushing it down in any way, use our intention to direct the pain out our base chakra. We can learn to move our energy in a healthy way, allowing every feeling, allowing ourselves to be the undefended heart, and being at peace.

We experience the losses and tragedies of life as painful, and although we may not be into articulating such a thing, we feel something like, "why me?" "This shouldn't be happening." We'll be able to let go of a lot of the pain of these situations by shifting our perception. First, as a human being living this life, we are going to lose loved ones, our children grow up, we lose our youth, we leave beloved places. It's all a part of a lifetime. We need to accept and meet these things from our knowledge that all things change. I don't mean that we should deny our human feelings about the loss of a certain form that our life has taken, but rather that we carry both levels of consciousness— human *and* spiritual. We can allow our feelings of loss while we also see the bigger picture of old forms shifting into the new. We can find the moment, where there is eternity. The hard pain of holding against loss then becomes the sweet pain of growth.

A wonderful practice is to hold an ideal for ourselves of the spiritual warrior who stands firmly and flexibly on his or her feet, allows the "lesson" to come in, gets the teaching, thanks the teaching, and then asks the universe to bring in the next one. This state of being allows the pain and keeps it in perspective. It allows the heart to be broken, and learns from it. This is the doorway to real safety.

> *"And God is always there, if you feel wounded.*
> *He kneels over this earth like a*
> *divine medic,*
> *and His love thaws*
> *the holy in*
> *us."*

ST. TERESA OF AVILA

CHILD/GODWOMAN—GODMAN:

The opening of a relationship between these two aspects of one's being is vital to our full healing.

The part of us that is the Godwoman/man is our mature adult consciousness connected to spirit that *must* be present for the wounded child as the good and wise parent who brings palpable love, support, acceptance and cherishing to the emotional wounding of the child. This aspect of healing must be in place to include the healing of our humanity in the walk to God, for it is a key. The child holds the emotional charge of the misconceptions in the soul.

At the level of the soul, the spiritual issues we have with the God-force are resolved by tracking into the disharmonies of our life, down and through into the level of general attitudes to life, and therefore, God.[45] For instance, we find deep beliefs that have been held in our unconscious, such as, "God is cruel," "God doesn't support." By connecting with our wisdom and love, we bring the Truth. At this stage of healing, a synergy develops between the healing process of the emotions in the child and the misconceptions in the psyche and the soul.

It is a crucial step for our healing to expand our consciousness into holding multiple states: wounded child, adult, spirit. This is integration that is necessary so we can apply what we know; so that we can embody kindness and brotherhood; so that we remember who we are.

> *"Dig here," the angel said –*
> *"in your soul,*
> *in your*
> *soul"*

ST. JOHN OF THE CROSS

---

45. See Format for Healing

EMOTIONS/FEELINGS:

Emotions are from the past. Feelings are in the present. Emotions are contracted energy. Feelings are fluid.

As previously discussed,[46] the parts of us that are hooked into the mass consciousness think our emotional reactions, those automatic negative emotions from our wounding, are the reality of who we are—what's really happening. Most of us reach maturity with deep wells of unexpressed pain and rage from our childhood that we have lost conscious contact with. On the other hand, if we're in touch with deep emotions, but tend to act out our pain or rage, we're stuck in a loop that doesn't touch the cause.

We also get stuck when we repress. We push the emotions down, below the level of our consciousness where they fester into emotional eruption or disease. These deep wells of unresolved emotions get tapped into when energies come at us that "hit the mark" of our wounding. We automatically become upset, angry, sad, overwhelmed in reaction.[47]

By contrast, feelings are the streamings of moving energy appropriate in the moment. We must have *all* our feelings available in order to be fully alive and to love deeply. In order to carry the state of full aliveness in the emotional body, we must empty out the repressed emotions, feel them fully, do the healing work, and through this process keep bringing ourselves back into emotional balance. If we don't open those closed-off places, the repressed energy will always leak out in some way—hurting ourselves, hurting others.

At a certain point in our healing, we enter a state of being where we are not ruled by our emotions anymore. We notice that we're having an emotional reaction and we can identify what it is and contain[48] it. We actually become more sensitive and can use our "reactions" as a guide to identify what's happening around us. For instance, "I'm feeling angry at this person and I don't know why. When I pay atten-

---

46. See Section 2, Blaming/Bliss
47. See Format for Healing
48. See Glossary

tion, I realize they are trying to manipulate me, my automatic reaction (fight back) came up, and I wasn't consciously aware of the trigger."

When our feelings are freely streaming, we can *allow* our sexual feelings to be present when they're present. We have a healthy attitude toward our sexuality, and aren't afraid we'll act out. We can contain our sexual feelings and enjoy them.[49]

Our emotional body needs to be open if we are to feel the deep love, not only in relationship but also on our spiritual path. If we are not *feeling* our connection and our love, our spirituality is only in our minds. Love is the foundational energy of the universe. And, if our feelings are not available,[50] we can't taste the experience of God.

There are two sources of the feeling experience: the Divine Self and our wounding. We have each in proportion to what is healed in us. For example, we may allow the streaming of feeling love and connectedness with regard to our children, but allow our partner only so close and no closer. To find the source of our feelings/emotions, we witness ourselves through the eyes of our heart, as much as we possibly can, and objectively assess whether the experience has an abiding quality, is integrous and contains the Truth of God. Is it dark or light? Contracted or flowing? Needy or giving?

Those experiences from our wounding have a quality of compulsion, coping and are highly subjective and charged, like a "rush."

A feeling experience from the Divine Self may be negative and the emotional wounding experience may have a positive emotion. For instance, the emotional experience of pride or vanity may feel good. By contrast the feeling response to perceiving a negative act may be unpleasant, even though the perception is sourced in Truth and the emotional body is open and flowing. There is no "cookie cutter" rule; we must practice paying attention.

As we become more emotionally mature, that is carrying the qualities of compassion, containment and self-responsibility, we can tolerate a broad spectrum of emotions/feelings and hold our Loving Witness with it all. We move into deeper and stronger alignment in our consciousness. The destructive and wounded inner child is ac-

---

49. See Section 2, Faithful/Unfaithful

50. See Processes, Working with Emotions

cepted, loved and healed by our inner loving parent, and does not act out; the mind is in service to the heart; sexual feelings are allowed and held as sacred. By emptying out our wells of repressed emotions, we become more congruent—our emotions are healed, we're not afraid of feeling anything that is in us; our feelings are consistent with our thoughts and actions.

Therefore, as we hold a wider spectrum of emotions and consciousness we can get up close and personal with our love. We can throw the caution of the contracted personality to the winds. We can participate on every level with our relationships and ourselves. There isn't a false faith or false love that always has a strong connotation of need. This more real place evolves from the true lover—a lover that brings through beauty, gratitude, honoring and compassion on all levels of consciousness, from physical through to the spiritual—with no safety net.

On a day when the wind is perfect
the sail just needs to open
and the love starts.

Today is such
a day.

RUMI

DISCERNMENT/JUDGE

The one is the harmonic of the other.

When we judge we can name a thing, but we put a value on it as right or wrong, good or bad. We all do this.

Not only do we have judgments, but also we believe that we have the right to act upon our opinion that someone's actions, words, thoughts, etc. are wrong or right. We have a good opinion of someone that we think is intelligent, or successful, or wears the right clothes or speaks the right language. However, we feel entitled to punish someone for being wrong/bad, and allow others to punish us for the same reason. We become judge, jury and executioner, and allow others to do the same.

No wonder we're afraid to reveal ourselves to each other! We're constantly watching to make sure we don't "slip up" and get caught in something that we'll be rejected or punished for. And, we're always watching to "catch" people. No wonder our relationships feel empty.

Before we can begin to heal the judge, we need to really let the Truth of the situation sink in. We separate from the other when we judge. We pull away and make ourselves better or worse—mostly better. Our pride comes in here, our comfort with being special. Our negativity gets acted out when we "rise above" the other and send hurtful criticisms through our thoughts, words or deeds (and, if we make ourselves the bad one or the wrong one, we become the "special" bad one—no one has ever been that bad!). When we hold someone "above" us, we are not happy for their success, etc.; we look for things to criticize and we lust after their power, wealth, beauty, etc.

Intrinsic in turning the judge "right-side-out" (returning the inverted, negative energy back to its harmonic state) is the full recognition and acceptance of the negativity in it. For instance, we have thoughts like: "That person is obese, so I know its true that they're messed up, self-indulgent, out of control"– and under the surface, we think/feel: "less than me." Even when we open our spirituality and do purification work, we can catch ourselves thinking thoughts like these and we immediately push it away and move to something pious. We sanitize it; make believe the judgment isn't really there. We don't usually name it it's true name, which alone is extremely powerful, and own that we still carry this stuff. By making someone bad and/or wrong, we decide that we possess more knowledge—that we're God from the ego– and that we have the right to demean. We have no idea of the journey of their soul—the bigger picture—how could we? So from our limited, puny perspective, we go into separation.

Waking up to the Reality of the judge is a deep step and requires that we put aside all our reasons and righteousness. The reasons are always the "booby" prize,[51] anyway. They are only justifications and excuses that numb us to what we are doing with our energy. That is re-

---

51. I heard this expression at the EST Training at or around 1978.

ally the only question of importance, "What am I doing?" Am I supporting or rejecting? Am I blaming or looking for love? If I'm using my energy to support and turn toward love, then I will not consider the transgressions of the other as so important. They made a mistake and I *interpreted* that as bad or wrong out of my wounding. When I choose to put down my sword and hold an attitude of connection toward the other, the "truth" changes from the truth of my personality to the Truth of my heart. The truth of the personality is the critic, judge, saboteur, princess, rebel, victim, the demanding child, etc.; the Truth of the heart is always inclusive and compassionate.

In healing the judge we also must begin to consciously train the mind—harnessing its clarity to do the work of the heart. This requires a commitment of the positive will to come in and stop the habitual lifelong pattern of ascribing a value to everything and everyone. (One of the deepest areas to go with this is to recognize that Mother was good and bad, Father too—and, then of course, me. Mother and Father represent our core experiences from which we project the "bad/good—right/wrong" forever after onto the world).

In healing the judge, we must find a deeper level of mind that witnesses what we think. As soon as we can observe that we're thinking a certain thing, or thinking in a certain way, we are in the witness. Most of our thoughts are an automatic tape of nonsense. If you watch them for a while, you will see that this is true.

A quality of the deep, Loving Witness is an ability to discern from clarity and non-judgment, and from a broad spectrum of awareness. Since this place is not hampered by contraction and myopia, it is able to see things that most people don't see.

> *"Judge not, that ye be not judged. For with what judgment ye judge, ye shall be judged; and with what measure ye mete, it shall be measured to you again. And why beholdest thou the mote that is in thy brother's eye, but considerest not the beam that is in thine own eye?"*[52]

---

52. St. Matthew 7: 1, 2, 3 (KJV)

CRISIS/CALM

When a crisis comes in, we tighten up. We think there's something wrong, terribly wrong. We blame someone, ourselves, God. We feel helpless in the face of circumstance. All of our doubts come up about ourselves, the universe we live in. Our emotions say, "there is no love, there is no help, there is only pain, disappointment, loss failure— in a word, darkness. If we look for it in our emotions, we'll find the belief that the substance of the universe is darkness and pain. We cringe from it, we try to tiptoe past it, and we have superstitions about it. There is, in fact, a belief held by the dark forces that there is no light. So, we know when that gloom comes up on our horizon, we're dropping into a low vibration—the world of darkness.

Another aspect of how we hold crisis as a disaster comes from a belief deep in the psyche that we're supposed to be happy. When things happen that catalyze anger, disappointment or pain, we scowl and move into an emotional attitude that translates into, there is injustice—God is unfair, an unjust old man in the sky. So when there's crisis, we want to push it away. We don't want to be responsible for anything. We want to stick our head in the sand. We want heads to roll. We want to run from any places inside us that are unhealed and carry an emotional charge of feeling worthless, bad, or wrong because a part of us knows that God is not unjust, so *we* must be at fault.

If we step back for a moment and think about the times of crisis in our lives, we realize that, although it was painful and difficult, something good came from it. Something inside us shifted. If we lost a loved one, perhaps the door to our spirituality opened a little wider through the recognition of impermanence; perhaps we allowed our feelings a little more and discovered the depth of our love. If we lost our income or a lot of money, perhaps we found a new direction or a resource of courage and creativity that would not otherwise have come forward. Perhaps we discovered the spiritual Truth that material things are not what bring us fulfillment.

As we heal and unlock our tight holding and wake up to the way this life works, we can pass "go" and collect our $200. We can allow flexibility when "things get rough" and our self-will gets thwarted, and look for what needs to be healed in us and what our lessons may be. There may still be a little part for a long time that bridles when the status quo is broken, but we learn to hold that contraction from the larger view. As we evolve still further, we can *welcome* the discomfort of the crisis knowing that it is the medicine for our healing and that as we look deeply, we will find the pearl in the chaos.

Viewing life's crises in this way is a quantum leap in consciousness. It's not merely behavioral modification, but rather a complete shift in how we hold our world. Life's difficulties become openings and, although we will still have places in our mind and emotions that will want to kick and scream, we have made the turn. The deeper part of us knows that the tendency to tighten up and grouse and complain is only illusion catalyzed by our past. If we practice looking into the crisis for the meaning underneath, we'll put into motion a positive vortex, which will take us into the depth of the peace in our heart. This is like living in the deep calm ocean, even while there may be a storm on the surface. We hold the crisis and the peace at the same time. We will attend to our wounded child, the outer events, and we'll be able to hear the Alleluia underneath.

> *"Crisis is an attempt of nature—of the natural, cosmic lawfulness of the universe—to effect change. Crisis in any form attempts to break down the old balance structures which are based on false conclusions and on negativity. It shakes loose ingrained, frozen life styles so that new growth becomes possible. It tears down and breaks up, which is momentarily painful, but transformation is unthinkable without it."[53]*

GOODNESS/BADNESS[54]

Well, this may seem like "Sunday School 101," but it truly is very deep when you think about it for a moment—not that some Sunday Schools aren't deep!

In our mentalized and sophisticated society it's considered naive

---

53. Pathwork Lecture #183, "The Spiritual Meaning of Crisis"
54. See Divinity/Inversion for an explanation of deeper levels of these energies

to talk about goodness and badness. The mass consciousness is more concerned with money, power, and the idolization of the intellect, and doesn't acknowledge anything it can't see, hear or touch. If we look beneath the surface, however, we discover that, not only are there goodness and badness, but there are evil and light. Evil is an old and unacceptable word in our world. When a person commits a heinous crime, we call it by psychological names: anti-social behavior or psychosis, or we blame the parents or the environment—both are half-truths. In our mentalized society we're afraid we'll be laughed at if we use the "e" word.

When we interact, we take part in the socially acceptable put-down that wants to undo the other; we malign, which puts an energetic knife in someone's back; we look for someone's weak spot and work it or hold it against them. Goodness is also an unsophisticated word. It's out of fashion in the mass consciousness to be a "good person." If it's said about someone today, it's probably with tongue-in-cheek.

When we begin to unhook from the "matrix" of the mass consciousness, however, our perspective changes. As we look at our inner tendencies, and as we watch the energy of what we do, we become aware that we *do* have negativity—we *do* hurt people. When we drop the whitewashing and excuses, the simplicity and power of the duality arises—it's either light or dark.

By the same token, we *do* help others and *are* kind. When we enter the purification process, we notice how difficult it is to manage those places that are less than good. A new picture begins to form. We realize that we're actually engaged in a "battle" with our own darkness. Even when we become aware of our negativities, they persist! That old concept we thought was superstition is actually true—there is a deep conflict between good and bad. As we discover the level of "badness" in others and ourselves there's only one word to describe it, evil.

The most superficial level of "goodness and badness" is connected with the consciousness that is centered in the earth plane—the realm of the third chakra.[55] This is the consciousness that believes only in the manifest world, and approaches being good or bad primarily from

---

55. See Additional Materials, Chakra Conscioiusness

a "mask" (false) place. This "mask" consciousness carries intent to look good to others, and to convince the self that you are a certain kind of "good" person so that you will be loved, admired, and validated. This "goodness" ends up being invasive, shallow, and disconnected. (For example, "oh, I love you so much I'm going to give you this self-help book that I know you need," or, "I am such a good person I'm going to try to force my beliefs on you," etc.) Real goodness has intent to give selflessly. This intent is a pure impulse that doesn't care about looking good, being right or getting something in return.

A person who is in touch with selflessness (not 100% there, but with a recognition of when there's ego attachment) does not act out on others. No matter what is going on inside—judgments, anger, hurt—there is intent to be a good person, and the right use of will which contains the negative impulses.

The way to cut through all the rationalizations for what we think, feel and do is to look squarely at our conduct. We often excuse our cynicism, hurtfulness, put-downs, etc. with rationalizations about why the other deserved it—they're bad and/or wrong. Or, we sugarcoat our remarks, gestures, facial expressions, so that it seems "such a small thing" that the negativity of it goes unconfronted. What happens here is that we close the feeling nature of our hearts.

At a deeper level in our psyche, we know what we are doing and feel guilty about it. We end up sabotaging and hating ourselves. We beat ourselves up in our own minds for our "infractions." We're afraid to look at the damage caused by the hurtful things we say and do because that will prove what we deeply fear to be the truth of who we really are, that our core is essentially "bad."

Once we begin to look at our behavior and hold an intention to do good from a pure place, we turn the tide karmically and energetically to the positive (for when you get the lesson, you release the karma). We relax deep inside and let go of the tightness that is afraid of being found out. We create a positive vortex of energy and bring ourselves into a higher vibration; we make a deep prayer. As you pay attention to this, you'll see that although "goodness" may be considered a kindergarten concept and something we all "know;" it is too seldom done genuinely from the heart.

This process of deep self-confrontation must come from "home base," our embodiment of our light. We all too often don't recognize (experience with our body, heart and mind) our real goodness when it's present. We make valiant efforts to be good and honest human beings in the face of deceit, put-downs, betrayal and judgments; we keep going against all odds and continue to give our understanding and support in the face of unkindness and harshness. We need to "see" our goodness and hold compassion for ourselves when we go "off," compassion rebalances everything.

> *A friend told me a story about the Dalai Llama, I can't authenti-*
> *cate it, but I share it because it has nourished my soul:*
> *A friend of this friend went to see the Dalai Lama at one of his*
> *events. She was sitting within the first few rows, so she could*
> *see him clearly. At one point, he made the comment, "It's so*
> *hard to be a good person," and there were tears running down*
> *his face.*

SELF-LOATHING/SELF-LOVE

Most of us aren't aware of hating ourselves. We also shy away from loving ourselves, lest we appear "egotistical."

The self-hatred comes into being from a disparity between who we think we should be and who we are. When we were children, we got the message that we weren't ok. We had to be in certain ways to get approval and love. So we developed the mask[56]-self, a false persona, to meet our world. As we grew up, we kept this false self and adopted it fully as whom we are. Our Real Self got pushed into our unconscious, which resulted in a denial of our authenticity, both light and dark. This process continues and has become so automatic that we've lost touch with what we're doing. We hide from ourselves. Therefore, when we think, feel, and act out in ways that don't meet our "standards" we rationalize so that our thoughts, emotions or behaviors fit with our false ideal. Unconsciously, however, we know when

---

56. See Glossary

we're thinking, feeling, acting, and speaking negatively and we judge ourselves for it.

When one of our faults shows, we cover it up, wall ourselves off from it psychically, and hate ourselves for having it. For example, you may hate your weakness, the part of you that "can't"[57] stand up for yourself. We cover it perhaps by withdrawal or "rising above." Or, we blame: our parents, the other, or the situation. When one of these unwanted parts get revealed, we "let it go by," without turning to healing, and we "forget" about it. We push it back and down into our unconscious and/or we ruminate about it until we've chewed it to shreds and it "disappears." This inner turmoil continues to live in our deep psyche and shows itself again and again when the button gets pushed. Eventually, the negative energy of the self-hatred moves into the tissues of the body, creating disease.

One way to access this level is to search out the ways that you punish yourself. Do you mistreat your body? Do you "harp" on your faults? Mistakes? Is the source of an illness possibly self-punishment? Is self-judgment the source of feeling poor? Is it the source of not having a loving mate? Where have you not forgiven yourself?

Forgiving ourselves for our faults is a necessary step in evolvement. This is often skipped over because it's so hard to do. We judge ourselves much more harshly than we judge anyone else.

There are different levels of forgiving yourself: one is for keeping the deep basic defense[58] in this lifetime, which constricts the heart and limits our capacity to love. Another place to forgive yourself is for those specific choices you've made that cause pain, to yourself and others. For instance, I chose to be a "modern" parent and not insist on sitting down to family meals together; I chose to "keep the peace" and not stand up for myself; I chose to use my body to barter for a good life; etc. As we age and reflect on our lives, we'll often judge and punish ourselves over and over again for making bad choices. I certainly have been there. This is a cruel and negative cycle with which we must do aikido. By this, I mean using the mistake, or the negative situation, for healing—recognizing the discomfort as a *signal* to find the teach-

---

57. Under "I can't" is always "I won't"

58. See Section 2, Offense/Defense

ing in it. (Discomfort of any kind signifies disharmony) For instance, I chose to use my body to barter for a good life" can be an excuse to hold contempt for yourself. Or, to do aikido,[59] we can look for the cause. (Perhaps you were raised to believe that physical beauty is all you're good for). We can have compassion for the young part that wasn't cherished for who you really are. We can bring in the Divine self to give that child what she really needs (acknowledgement and acceptance). Then, to bring in the full healing, look to the spiritual teaching—remembering that from God we're always honored, never used.

Self-hatred also shows itself through procrastination. You don't do what's healthy, right, needed and good because "something" just comes in and keeps you from it. That "something" is an anti-life energy of immobility that feeds on your negativity. And, the truth of the energy is that we're *choosing* to sabotage ourselves. Not only do we sabotage ourselves from a wound, but also we unconsciously know what we're doing and hate ourselves for it.

A cover-up for self-hatred is hatred of others. The negative view in which we deeply hold ourselves gets projected outward.

We don't have to take that well-worn path and reject ourselves for our weakness and faults. When we see deeply into what we're doing and why,[60] we can turn our focus to find the love, the harmony. In loving ourselves, we don't go to the opposite pole from self-hatred to self-indulgence and denial of our negativity. We bring our positive intentionality forward to expand and hold *all* of who we are, from compassion. We bring our intention to self-forgiveness and at the same time accept that we have darkness. When I find myself in self-judgment, I ask, "Am I willing to I love myself this way?"

The willingness to be honest with ourselves brings self-respect and self-love.

"Where do you love your soul, your mentality, your body?"[61]

---

59. See Glossary
60. See Format for Healing
61. Pathwork Lecture #240, "Aspects of the Anatomy of Love: Self-love, Structure, Freedom"

AFFIRMATIONS/GOING BACKWARDS

An important aspect of entering mastery of the ego involves train-ing the mind and emotions as well as entering into full acceptance of our spiritual selves and our power to create. Affirmations are a useful tool to help us remember our spiritual nature as we learn to manage our wandering thoughts and immature emotions. It's quite a leap to awaken to the fact that we are *not* our emotions or our thoughts, but something deeper than has consciousness and can witness with compassion this journey we've undertaken. We walk through a portal into another reality when we begin to get that distance from the wild and wooly world of compulsive, disturbing thoughts and emotional reactions that seem to dictate what we say and do. This place is ever at choice, calm, serene and centered in our deep, Loving Witness. What a different world we enter! This world turns out to be more truly us than our fears and insecurities.

We deeply want to affirm this new reality that we're discovering: that we are lighted, powerful, loving creators—and more. We can talk to those errant parts of us that want to think the worst and "get the other guy," and tell them who's boss. We have the capacity to tell our mind and emotions what it is we want to focus on, what kind of day we're going to have. We can wake up and affirm, "I am powerful and loving, and I'm going to come to this new day with gratitude, appreci-ation, and a loving spirit." It's not a magic pill, but a volitional ignition of our highest impulses, even though there may be uncomfortable emotions or thoughts in the background—or even in the foreground. It's a choice of who will be driving the bus. This is the beginning of freedom. This is the beginning of making the deep prayer of turning our energies toward love.

As we call forth beautiful words and loving intention, we affirm the Reality of God's truth. We energetically bring into our field a higher vibration. On the spiritual level, we're taking another step into harmony. On the mental level, we absolve our wrong beliefs and rec-ognize Truth. On the emotional level, we open our hearts to peace and joy. On the physical level, we let go of the deep holding that we all unconsciously do against the vagaries of life.

If you come to your affirmations with this congruency of the levels of your being, you'll move forward. However, if you're using affirmations and not doing your inner work, trying to escape life and yourself, or are in denial, you'll feed the contraction and make it stronger by keeping it hidden. You'll also live in an illusory spirituality of the mind—you will go backwards.

> *"If you find yourself in a hole,*
> *the first thing to do is stop digging."*
>
> COWBOY PROVERB

FAITHFUL/UNFAITHFUL

Most of us believe that "faithful" is good and "unfaithful" is bad. Of course, there is the secret belief that unfaithful is ok, as long as nobody knows. Most of us are, however, in judgment of unfaithful behavior, or at least we acknowledge that society makes it bad, undesirable. Where do the boundaries lie, though? If we let go of society's rules and ask with our full, adult, awake mind, "What do we really mean by faithful? Unfaithful?" Ultimately, we all have to answer these questions for ourselves in our own heart. As we look deeply, we want to be as clear as possible and free from distortions arising from our fears. If we're willing to be honest about what our real issues are around commitment, the clouds begin to disappear and our emotional beliefs come to the surface.

We may fear that if we commit, the other will control us, take away our fun and our freedom. We may fear that by committing we must allow them to act out their negativity on us. We may be afraid they'll steamroll us. Perhaps we don't want to let go of the "rush" we get when we know someone outside our relationship is interested in us.

In the recesses of our deep psyche, we don't believe we have any control, we believe that others are malevolent and will hurt us; we believe that we're not of value. These emotional beliefs need to be brought out into the light of awareness so we can get some clarity, and thereby heal. If we keep defending, we'll continue to make it about the other person and never get to the core. We'll continue to take the path of least resistance and won't find the freedom and growth that can come from within the structure of total and full commitment to one human being. If we take the plunge into the pool of being in our "yes" to the other, and are met by a "yes," we can climb to great heights of love, courage, understanding, and experience the bliss of merging.[62]

If the "Eros" stage—the honeymoon—is drawing to a close and we look at the person we love and see that they are a good, balanced, mature, kind and loving individual, then we may choose to begin the work of deep loving. This means that we accept that relationship is a path to God; we accept that the friction is a good thing. It's there so we can find the places in us that are contracted and in misconception (wounded).

If we can hold an attitude of good will and compassion for the other and ourselves in this process, we've found the doorway to intimate relating.

Too often, we think that the "Eros" stage is supposed to last and we get disappointed when it begins to fade. The reality is that we can keep the Eros alive by working at the relationship, committing fully and being willing to reveal ourselves. Initially, we have to delve deeper into our emotional reality about what "full commitment" means to us, our fears and our expectations.

To commit fully, we're willing to trust the other with our finances, family, lifestyle (the willingness to blend and bend), heart-connected sexuality, and to hold the relationship as a field within which to grow. That is, this person is a stand-in for God and my relationship to him shows me where I'm surrendered and where I'm not. It's not the genie that makes us happy at last—although supreme happiness most definitely can happen if we're present in our adult consciousness and aren't demanding happiness from the child.

If we're not willing to open every corner of our lives completely to the other, there is no foundation. If one area is faulty or not present, there's always a question—verbalized or not—as to whether or not there's a pad from which to launch. It's really very simple, and it's very hard to do. Many, many, if not most, relationships don't even approach

---

62. See Glossary

these levels of openness and strength. People think they "know" the other; they've "got their number." They then react forever after to the very limited spectrum of the other person that they have decided is all there is. And, again for the most part, they're reacting out of their own wounding that pastes on to their partner people and situations from the past. The fact is we can never know another human being fully. By choosing a limited spectrum of behavior and experience with ourselves and the other, we think/feel we're safe in a cocoon of "knowns" and live out our lives on automatic pilot, i.e., running away from life and intimacy.

One of the first things to do as we reevaluate who we are and who we want to be in relationship, is to take a hard look at what we really believe in our hearts and what's been force-fed to us from the outside. The mass consciousness in our society holds within it low-vibratory attitudes that promote separation as an illusion of safety. Around finances it says something like, "well, I have a lot more than this other person, it's only right that they should give up any claim to my assets." Around family, "well, his family is uneducated, poor, too controlling, arrogant, misguided—so, I'll feel superior and be aloof." Around lifestyle, "well, this guy doesn't know how to live well, he has no taste, I'll teach the right way." Around sexuality, "well, I like be free to have fun with the opposite sex, it's innocent, and my sexuality is mine not hers." Around growth, "well, I don't need any funky therapy or psychobabble about relationship; it's better to just be yourself." Ooh, la, la, a bunch of half-truths! What about,

> *"How*
> *Did the rose*
> *ever open its heart*
> *and give to this world all of its beauty?*
> *It felt the encouragement of light against its being,*
> *otherwise we all remain too*
> *frightened."*

> HAFIZ

So, when we come back to the traditional meaning of "faithful" and "unfaithful," we look at sexuality. If we're looking at the state of being that holds as true only what we can see, feel, or touch, then faithfulness is physical. "As long as there isn't penetration, I'm not being unfaithful." If you're aware that emotions also create reality, then you would include having sexual feelings and body sensations with someone else as unfaithful. If you know that thoughts create emotions and reality, then you would include having lustful thoughts as unfaithful. If we use our mental energy to fantasize about having sex with other people and allow our emotions to attach to this, we're living in a netherworld and missing the extraordinary beauty of being fully present with this person in this incredible moment, now.

When you're in the state of being that takes responsibility for your thoughts, emotions and actions, you realize that the real indicator of unfaithfulness is *intention* and *how you use your energy*. If sexual energy is engaged—no matter on what level: physical, emotional, mental or energetic—with someone besides your partner, then you are leaking[63] vital life force. Sexual energy gets sent out to toy with the other, to pump up your ego, and with a disregard for the emotional state of the other person. If that other person wants you and you're not willing to reciprocate, the exchange is punishing to them. Also, the relationship you're in gets undermined. Your actions decode as, "I'm not ready to choose one person," or "I want to keep you off balance," or "I need this feeling of power more than I need you."

Energetically, sexual energy comes through our eyes, body language, words, intonation, as well as the purely physical. When I look at flirtation clairvoyantly, I see ribbons of energy from the groin reach out and wrap themselves around the sexual organs of the other. These ribbons of energy also come out of the eyes and hands. Even if we prove our fidelity to ourselves by *not* having physical sex, the bottom line is that we're still *misusing our energy*—we're still acting out energetically.

Discovering that you may use your sexual energy inappropriately doesn't mean that you must shut it down most of the day and open up only when your partner is around. The healthy sexual energy remains open and flowing. You're aware that other people, flowers, animals, even the soft breeze is sensual and sexual. You can, of course, ex-

---

63. See Glossary

perience in a healthy way being turned on by someone other than your partner, or a waterfall, or the wind in your hair. The difference is engagement. If you mix it up with someone else on any level, you're feeding a wound in you and you're not being faithful to your partner. A foundational part of your relationship has a wobble.

The answer is that this behavior—while you're in relationship—comes from a wound. *The wound is the root of the matter.* And, looking for the wound is the only way out of the dilemma. It can be poor self-esteem, lack of confidence, fear of losing your partner so you leave first, belief that you can't have pleasure, fear of annihilation, etc. We can find this by tracking the emotions present when we're "straying." If we decode these, we'll be on our way to the root issue.[64]

Fidelity also comes from the capacity to be faithful to oneself. This doesn't mean that we run roughshod over others because "that's my truth," or "that's what I need right now." That is a misuse of self-care. Deep personal fidelity is the strength to be honest with ourselves and at the same time having compassion for our errant behavior. It's commitment to carrying the intention of staying faithful to the highest that is in me.

The truest and most important level is the spiritual level. Committing to one other without reservation opens the door to continually search the vastness of the other to forever discover their amazing and beautiful complexity. When we let go of defending our heart, our deepest issues can come to the surface. When there's no back door, no safety valve, we enter the lapidary of full-on relationship where we get to witness our strengths, beauty, and virtues and deal with the hurts of our childhood and the misconceptions in the soul, which are mirrored in the relationship. By letting go of any pseudo-protection and surrendering to at least one other human being; giving the gift of commitment and fidelity, we can meet our terror of merging, with ourselves, the other and with God.

As we look at fidelity, we meet our sexuality in a deep way. Our attitudes around our sexuality hold an important key to our life issues. Through our ongoing sexual fantasies,[65] we can find our deepest

---

64. See Format for Healing
65. See Processes, Working with Sexual Fantasies

wounds. Everything else in our lives is present in our sexuality. It's a window through which we can heal everything.

Sexuality is personal and cosmic. At the base chakra level it's for procreation and physical pleasure, at the second chakra it's for connection, at the third chakra it's to discover the other, from the fourth (heart) and the spiritual chakras above it's for total integration and merging with the self, the other, and God. Sexuality is meant to bring the Divine through the elemental physical body…to spiritualize the material.

When we hold our sexuality in this way it becomes a sacred thing. It's a sacred thing that we share with the one we love. When we hold our sexuality in this way, "faithful" becomes a natural extension of a loving, full-on relationship with the right use of our thoughts, emotions, body and energy. Built on this foundation, the heart and spirit can soar.

Rumi says, "the way you make love, is the way God will be with you."

SPECIALNESS/ORDINARINESS

We all mightily need our specialness, so we can have *something* in this life. Most of us are all too aware of our weaknesses and faults, our imperfections, our mistakes, our fears. If we're not special, different, better in some way—secretly, in the recesses of our mind—we are surely worthless.

The need to be special comes out of our wounding as children. No matter what the circumstances of our family of origin, we get the message that our authenticity is not acceptable. Out of this come feelings of unworthiness. To cover this up and to seek the love and acceptance we need, we strive to be "more" and "better"—special.

We may find our specialness in illness, in our intellect, our emotions, our objectivity, our body, our misery, our talent, our spirituality, and on and on. These feelings and states of being, if not conscious, are just beneath the surface of our awareness in our subtle emotional currents.

To be special we must be separate. So, while we're "taking care" of our feelings of worthlessness, we languish in loneliness. We may try to cover the loneliness with lots of activity and "friends," but we can't shake that sense of unfulfillment and hollowness that comes from being cut off. Our natural state is connection. When we feel connected, our personality feels fulfilled and our soul is in harmony. Our deepest wound is separation from God.

Finding this existential worthlessness breaks the pattern of the separateness and the holding against being found out. It opens the door to our wholeness. Once we find the source of the need to be special, the childhood wounding and unresolved needs, we can have mercy for ourselves. We can find our true worth as a part of God. We can step off our pedestal—that lonely and tortured place—and join the human race. We accept the fact that we're ordinary. This movement brings a fulfillment and peace we haven't known.

When we heal to a certain degree of integration, we meet our uniqueness. As we let go of the specialness and allow ourselves to be like everybody else, we concurrently become aware of our uniqueness. We discover the jewels we've been carrying that we weren't aware of, our capacity to love, the inner safety, and the connection. This is a Real experience, not a part of our wounding that *needs* to be better, but a deep recognition of our true nature and the nature of the universe.

We may still hear the disconnected voices: "you're a fool," "they're stupid," they're inept," "I really *am* better," and on and on, but now we know they're in illusion. We can come in for ourselves and hold the conviction to walk the razor's edge, "this voice is not in reality, and I'm not going with it."

As we hold the paradox of being ordinary and unique, we discover our magnificence—an experience our "specialness" could only dream of! We've entered a new Reality, one that's inclusive. From this place we meet the world from our ordinariness and our magnificence, both. This is the state of being that is at once a master[66] and a beginner. This is the one who is extraordinarily ordinary.

---

66. See Glossary

*"...I like that free feeling when
the line gets crossed from the
bondage of being somebody
into being wide open."*

ROBERT K. HALL

DEPENDENCE/INDEPENDENCE

Dependence and Independence are polar opposites. If we're dependent, we have a belief that we need someone else to make life ok for us. If we're independent, we have a belief that there is no help anyway, so I'll do it myself, thank you very much! Both ends of this pole are in misconception. Neither of these states is in reality. Reality is in the middle—it's autonomy. The consciousness of autonomy knows that we must stand with a strong spine, do our part, and meet life. It also knows that we are inextricably interconnected, so we can ask for help and know that it'll be forthcoming at the same time that we know we can meet life on our own. This is the balance of the polarities of dependence and independence. As long as we're still strongly influenced by our wounding, it's very difficult to find balance emotionally, and we keep bouncing back and forth from one pole to the other.

We tend to think of ourselves as either end of a polarity. First, we need to find one end, and then we need to find the other end, because we carry both. Examining different areas of our life will show us how we meet them. For instance, we may tend to be submissive a lot in our relationships. Once we see that, we would need to look for the opposite pole, our megalomania. When we've found both emotionally as well as mentally, we automatically move toward center—appropriateness of response. We don't have to be 100% there, we need just enough clarity of experience to notice what that balance *feels* like. When we know what we're doing and why, we can step back and work on bringing ourselves back to center.[67]

In order to deeply understand the healed energy, we must be able

---

67. See Format for Healing

to connect to those places where we *are* autonomous, to recognize what we have.

As we move more and more into autonomy, for it's a process, we can even choose to allow ourselves to be dependent on others for certain things. All the while, knowing that we can do it for ourselves. When we break free from the co-dependence of needing another person so we can feel legitimate, in control, protected, taken care of, important, beautiful, etc., we can then give a beloved the gift of saying, "I will depend on you for this or that." This is *allowing* another to enter your life.

From this place, you'll draw someone who can meet you. Then magic happens.

"A disease known is half cured."

IRISH PROVERB

OFFENSE/DEFENSE

Most of the world plays out this game—I push for my way or I defend against attack. It goes on and on, in a vicious cycle. Peace can only come when we refuse to fight.

Before we can put down our sword, however, we need to see, feel and know the sword. We need to find out why we picked it up in the first place and then recognize the futility of the fight. The fight channels our energies into a negative spiral. It strengthens the contraction of our misconceptions, inhibits our ability to be in compassion, keeps our vibration from refining, and allows our darkness to stay hidden. It keeps us from the deepest longing of our heart—to merge, to find the bliss of no-problem, safety, the truth, happiness, loving and being loved that is the harmony of oneness.

Where do our defenses come from? In order to understand, we need to start at the deep level of the soul. Our soul is a *conscious* energy that never dies. It's a part of the enduring harmony of the cosmos. The consciousness of our soul wants to learn—wants to eat of the fruit of the tree of knowledge, and we learn by experience. If someone talks about abandonment, for instance, we intellectually understand the concept, but if we've been abandoned in some way, we "know" it in our cells.

At a certain point, we began a journey into the void to experience. As we entered denser and denser energy, levels of our "oneness and harmony" began to break apart and move into duality. We broke into two sexes, our emotions and body split from our mind; our heart split from our sexuality; we also split into: wise-naive; child-adult; royalty-pauper; judge-victim; kind-cruel; etc., etc. We traveled into the density until we were in so much pain that we made the choice to turn to the light. We began the journey back home. This is where we are now on this earth-plane, we've made it to the level of 50% light-50% dark. On this earth plane, the energies are not as dense as in other levels we've passed through, and there is equal opportunity to go either way—light or dark. We can make a "case" here for either reality, and are at deep choice point.

As we're ready to incarnate into each lifetime, many of us meet with our guides to plan what lessons we'll focus on for this life. (Those that are not ready to participate in this process are given their tasks by their guides). When we incarnate, a veil comes down as to the level of our true expansion, so that we can focus on the issues at hand. If we knew how magnificent and lighted we are, we wouldn't have much motivation to face the pain of learning. You know how we humans are, when we're happy we don't work too much on ourselves. It's only when we're in sufficient pain that we'll stop, look inside and get the teaching.

As we enter the family that's handpicked to stimulate our misconceptions about the nature of Reality, we become impacted by our parents and living circumstances.

They impact us in just the right way so that we can experience the feeling, as well as the mental and spiritual dimensions of our misconception.

The impact from our parents is overtly slight or strong, depending upon what our soul needs to receive as stimulus. For example, we may have a misconception that God is unloving. Therefore, our parents may not want us and reject us at every turn; or we may encounter a milder version where we experience only one parent who tends to be aloof. In either case, the receptor site (the misconception in the soul) for this energy gets activated and the belief that we are not loved is carried in the mind, emotions and body.

In order to cope with the pain, we pull from our Divine qualities something we can use to "protect" us emotionally from the experience we dread. We tighten up on every level as this "protection" solidifies. Gradually, the pain of the childhood wounding gets pushed into the unconscious and we go through life cut-off and separate, but feeling "safe," and superior.

We may say, "Oh, I had a wonderful childhood. There was no real pain in it; just the usual kid stuff." It's true, however, that if there is any disharmony in your life now, it's self-evident that there's something unresolved in your childhood.

The three major essence qualities that we pull on for our defenses are Love, Wisdom and Power. We have all three qualities, but usually one is more predominant and provides the energy that gets misused for our "favorite" system of protection.

If we come in with a strong essence of Wisdom, we'll feel most comfortable pretending to be peaceful. We shut off our feelings because they lead to pain, we bring our awareness into our head—our lower mind—and we convince ourselves that we're not really affected by others or the circumstances of life. Whenever we even get a whiff of the old pain coming, we cut off our feelings and move into "objectivity." Since we're not emotionally available to the people in our lives, we inadvertently create what we want to avoid the most—the disconnect (loneliness, and a sense of not being loved).

When we realize that we have this defense, it is the very devil (so to speak) to heal it. We're attached to it. We "grow" into liking it and want to keep it. We make our aloofness into something we're proud of, "this is the way people *should* be." So, most of our lives we keep giving it energy and create a strong energetic form in our field that we habitually interact with unconsciously and automatically.

In the process of healing and allowing the pain to rise to the surface, a spectrum is traversed from being unconscious to what's happening, hence living in isolation and projecting an energy of false serenity, to the free flow of feelings, the courage to connect and the full embodiment of divine serenity that is filled with wisdom, love and power.

The next major defense comes from the essence quality of Power. Hence, this person is learning about power predominantly in this lifetime, and the will to be powerful and in control is paramount. This energy seeks to dominate and have *power over*. (The passive form of this defense is the victim—who is always in control). The turn to aggression is ignited by a childhood wounding of not being seen, heard or understood. Having power over is an attempt to force the world (parents/God) to see, hear and understand them. When we look at this clearly, we can see that, of course, they will push people away and not get what they need.

In order to heal, it's essential that feelings of helplessness be allowed to come to the surface. Through feeling their helplessness, the childhood pain is experienced and released, and the person discovers that real power is merged with love and wisdom.

The third defense is submission. It comes from the wound of deprivation when the parents love the child but don't express it (perhaps one or both are repelled by the physical), hence there's little or no pleasure in being loved. This child believes that in order to have pleasure, *everyone* must love me *all* the time. This child equates being loved and taken care of as the way to have pleasure. A characteristic of this defense is submitting to be cared for (an unspoken contract). The submission defense is characterized by an imbalance in the emotions. It causes people to turn away because they don't want to be manipulated.

It's essential for healing that they allow their rage. Through the opening of the rage that's held inside, the hurt of the past can be released and the strong essential quality of love can be experienced in a real way.

The defenses are an illusory house of cards that can topple at just the slightest touch, so we put a lot of energy into maintaining a state of hyper-alertness to any threat that might disturb our "reality." We live in a constant state of tension deep within the body, mind and emotions. We're so used to it that we don't even know it's there. We get a hint when we're sick, or something big happens and we let go of the tight control. Only then do we realize that we've been wound up tighter than a spring.

Within the structure of our defense, there's a place where darkness gets attached. We grew up, are out of the painful situation and yet keep choosing the contraction of our defense over and over. We have to take responsibility for our negative choices and their concurrent emotional rush: "I *like* feeling better than you," "I *like* running roughshod over you," "I *like* manipulating you," "I *like* closing my heart." We need to notice where the darkness in our defense is acted out on the crucible of "the issue." (That is, under the story of what was said and done, there is a level of consciousness that loves the fight and "getting" the other).

This is where we enter the territory of our lower self.[68] There's a part of our lower self that's at the level of negativity—hurtfulness, superiority, etc., and there is the deeper level that hates and destroys. There's even a negative pleasure in the "going with the dark." There's a place we can't whitewash with ersatz positive motives, but must look at squarely in the eye. Our negativity is largely unconscious, and finding it is hard on our made-up self-image.

We generally have a mixture of defense patterns. There is usually a primary "favorite' and a secondary defense. The third is present, but not so prominent. Often different defenses are used in different circumstances. We may meet the world mostly by going to our mind, but with our family we tend to submit and be full of emotion. We might tend to aggress only rarely.

Dismantling our defenses is a process over time because we have made it a strong habit, and also because ripping away the "protection" from the wounded child can be devastating. It takes time to bring those tender places into healing. It also takes work, and courage, recognition and acceptance, then commitment, perseverance, and a deep desire to heal your heart. Although we face painful places in this process, the pain experienced in healing is a sweet pain. And, as we heal the contracted "protection" of the wounded child consciousness, we inevitably turn to "What else can protect me?"

As we observe ourselves and our tendencies, bring healing to the child, give up the fight, choose and put into action loving ways of being, we can begin to experience the essential quality more than it's defensive inversion. We become aware of, and initiate, the blending

---

68. See Glossary and Processes, Working with the Lower Self

and balancing of love, wisdom and power. The three energies begin a synergy: Power becomes transformed and deeply embodied when infused with Love and Wisdom. It becomes understood as a part of a triumvirate, and the realization arises that real Power is a part of the whole, and power over is an illusion. Love is enhanced and balanced by Wisdom and Power. It expands with the Christ Consciousness. Wisdom becomes heartfelt and strong in the merging with Love and Power. With the help of our guides and the myriad forces of the Divine, we bring the three energies together for wholeness. Then we can walk our path from a place where the consciousness driving the bus is largely healed. From that alignment, we can meet the loving and negative energies that come toward us from a flexible, strong, heartfelt state of being—the Divine—The Loving Witness.

It's not that we don't know what the healed energy feels like. There's a large part of all of us that *is* healed. We *do* experience deep love. We just need to know that's who we really are.

"There is a light seed grain inside.
You fill it with yourself, or it dies."

RUMI

HURT/SAFETY

So often some small incident, a few words spoken, can feel like a grave personal insult. Sometimes, it's a certain kind of person who says a certain kind of thing. Sometimes, it's someone we live with or are close to that has a way about them that feels hurtful to us. We nurse these hurts for days, weeks, even years. When another hurts us, deep inside we *know* that they meant to. We *know* that they were aware of our tender spot and "went for it." We believe that they consciously "wanted" to hurt us. We build a "case" piece by misguided piece until we see them only through the distorted lens of one character trait or one incident. Or, we hold it silently against them forever. We think we have justified reactions—that *anybody* would do the same. Over and over again this happens, and we continue to give energy, consciously or unconsciously, to the belief that people will always hurt us. The world is not safe.

And, by the same token, when we hurt someone—if we're lucky and they let us know—we never "meant" to. Or, we believe they're being "too sensitive." We feel and act as if they are "off the wall," and "shouldn't feel that way." In truth, we're not in touch with the other or ourselves. .

Under the surface of "he said, she said," when we're hurt, we're actually reminded of something from our past and are reacting to it. We enter the emotional/mental/physical experience of our wounding that creates a distorted view of the situation in the now. We turn to a "tried and true" coping mechanism of running away, aggressing, or submitting. We keep our focus outward, on the other person and blame, blame, blame. Or, perhaps, we go into denial and say, "Oh, she's just strong willed, she didn't mean it that way." Whatever defensive course we take, it doesn't work because we get hurt anyway, and we end up closing down our hearts and hiding from the Truth.

The place we have to look when we get hurt is not outward, but rather to our history. "Is this situation and feeling familiar?" "Has it happened repeatedly in my life?" "Was I hurt with this kind of energy when I was a child?"[69]

As we work with the inner child and heal the emotions and misconceptions, we're less likely to fall into that familiar pit of emotional reaction from the past. We learn how to bring in our Godwoman to that young and vulnerable part of us and give the protection that's sorely needed. The adult/spiritual self creates the safety. The "child" no longer has to try to get safety from others. He no longer has to use his defense to create the illusion of safety, that's really not safe at all.

Of course, we'll continue to feel hurt sometimes and we don't heal everything at once, but when we can recognize our signal[70] that we're in the past, our wounded child doesn't have to take the energy and we're not getting re-traumatized.

Safety comes from the inside. Hurt is from our history. (If we

---

69. See Format for Healing
70. See Glossary

didn't have the "stupid button," and someone insinuated that we were stupid, we would laugh).

In addition to the healing of our history, we must make friends with the fact that there *is* pain in the world. If we close off and contract to "protect" our heart from rejection and loss, we never really live. So, when we're 102 and sitting in the rocking chair on the porch looking back at our life choices, what will we feel good about?

Our adult knows that she can take care of whatever comes. Our Higher Self knows that we're in reality spirit that can never be harmed, and that the body is the earthly shell through which we receive many of our teachings. So surrender to the hurt, let it move through and out, learn from it. Heal your history. Trust your process. Find your safety in the moment.

> "Be kind to yourself, dear—to our innocent follies.
> Forget any sounds or touch you knew that did not help you dance.
> You will come to see that all evolves us."
>
> RUMI

BAD HABITS/GOOD HABITS

We're all aware of those "bad habits" that we don't take too seriously—eating sugar, not exercising, not changing the oil in our car. We know these negative things we do or don't do can cause damage, but we know also that we're making the choice. Even though we're conscious to them, we need to track to the source and find out what's really going on.[71] We're not just weak or undisciplined; there are deeper causes.

There are those habits that are hurting us, however, that we're *not* aware of.

The unconscious habitual patterns can have far-reaching affects, and can literally run our lives. We think we're in control, making choices and evaluating what's happening, but the deeper truth is that we are, sometimes to a great extent, out of control. Or, to be more

---

71. See Format for Healing

precise, there is a powerful unconscious part of us that creates an "automatic" reaction, and we're not at choice in certain circumstances and with certain people. Even those people with aggressive energies that appear proactive are in fact automatically reacting to a belief that the world is hostile and must be controlled.

We think it's the way of things that the world aggresses upon us and "what everybody does" is react in specific ways. We don't think about it, we just react, "you insult me, and I insult you back." Until we begin to wake up to the deeper habits of automatic reacting to the world in a set way, we're asleep to our power of creation and choice. And, we act out negativities that, if we thought about it, we would never do. Part of "waking up" is the recognition of these unconscious and semi-conscious "dictates."

These habits that we are unaware of, and that we feed constantly by "going with them," create an energetic form in our field that we interact with all the time. We give it energy and it ignites us, back and forth, back and forth. It gets stronger and our habitual pattern gets set, as if in concrete. The first order of business is to become aware of these habitual patterns. That's 50% of the work. We need to look deeply and discover the inner cause of the habit.[72]

The habitual pattern builds up a momentum and it's necessary to break that momentum. It takes awareness, strength and perseverance to do this. The habitual pattern carries a compulsion with it. So, we must understand what's happening and why.[73] Then, we bring in our positive will to handle the compulsion and stop the momentum of the well-worn path of thought, emotion, and action. This interruption is carried out by the adult, healed ego *infused with spirit*. We turn the "bad habit" inside out and bring in the "good habit"—the seed of the Divine. If the bad habit that was formerly unconscious is to discipline your child from your undisciplined anger, you would need to be conscious when you're going into it, stop it, and replace the undisciplined anger by containing[74] your emotions and connecting to the loving

72. Ibid
73. Ibid
74. See Glossary

teacher in you. This is not an easy thing to do. It requires the spiritual warrior.

This needs to be worked from the opposite end also. That is, from the positive "spiritual practice."[75] It is important to do this from a commitment to practice compassion, because we find ourselves in the middle of the undesirable pattern again and again. The intention to embody compassion is a deep learning and practice in itself. It's a part of our mission in life to bring through our vehicle (body/mind/ emotions/spirit) the goodness and connection that are essential qualities of the Godforce. When we cut the bad habit "off at the pass," we create an inner dignity and respect for ourselves. We infuse daily occurrences with light. We find that we're actually happy because we're congruent and following the highest and best that's in us. Happiness becomes a good habit.

"The Chinese say that water is the most powerful element, because it is perfectly nonresistant. It can wear away a rock and sweep all before it."

FLORENCE SCOVEL SHINN

WHOLE TRUTH/HALF-TRUTH

How we get tripped up here! There are whole realms of darkness dedicated to the half-truth that "hooks" us with its piece that feels right.

When there's a half-truth, we have, perhaps, a subtle awareness that something isn't quite right, but we generally let it go by. This is an area where we need to pay attention and be present in the moment to exactly what's happening. We have to decode the "uneasiness." For instance, if I say, "I love you and want the best for you, so I have to tell you that your husband really should get a proper job." Well, there we sit across from our mother, father, or best friend and we know that they truly love us. However, what's being said under the surface is:

---

75. Ibid

"I love you and I have a judgment about your life." But, the advice is unasked for and from a judgment, and the whole truth is: there may be a problem that you need to look at, and the advice giver is hiding their negativity behind their love—half-truth.

Another instance may be a wife or mother who says, "I accept you as you are" but doesn't confront drug use. There is a spiritual truth here: accept what is, but it uses this truth to take the path of least resistance—to be co-dependent. One I catch myself using is, "I'll just follow my energy today." The truth part is that it's good to listen to your body and follow your intuition, but it shouldn't be used to allow escape from doing things you don't like. We have to listen closely. We have to question our motives, not in a neurotic way that's hyper-alert and unsure of ourselves, but from the place of knowing ourselves well enough to catch our negative tendencies.

In order to differentiate between a whole truth and a half- truth, we have to be able to look at ourselves with courage and honesty, and be willing to see things that we consider undesirable. Because of our denial, often our energies are mixed, both positive and negative. For example, we may be harboring a judgment about someone's taste when we're commenting on their new couch. Consciously, we're trying to say something "nice," but the judgment we have underneath will show in a subtle way—an intonation in the voice, a look in the eye, a tilt of the head. Something will "give it away." When that happens, the person will always react to our negative energy, not our positive. We will wonder why they withdraw or make a negative comment.

If we're totally honest with ourselves about our negativity, we won't be afraid to look at anything in ourselves or outside. We'll know the whole truth when its present, and we'll also recognize half-truth. We won't be blindsided by energies that slide under our radar. Where we're blind to parts of ourselves—both light and dark—we'll be blind to those energies in the world.

We learned as children to deny our negative impulses and we were conditioned to rationalize them—"A little put-down is just a joke!" We develop an "idealized self"[76] that we fiercely cling to and defend, so we don't want to see ourselves as a negative person. We

---

76. See Glossary

must confront the fear[77] within in order to see through the smoke of the half-truth.

If we're willing to look at our prejudices, our judgments, our vested interests, and if we're able to understand and embrace the wounding beneath, we'll be able to ask ourselves, "What is the *whole* truth here?" "What's my higher intent and what's my lower intent?" and we'll know the difference between the "truth" of our judgments: "You really should go on a diet, you know!" our wounding" "If you loved me, you wouldn't hurt my feelings." and the Truth of God—the whole truth, the loving Truth.

In my opinion, some of the greatest spiritual teachings are put forth from a context of half-truth. The idea that God[78] judges when we do right from wrong is a half-truth. God is presented as a old man in the sky that watches like a mean-spirited parent who holds a yardstick of what is good, he'll "reward" you; and when he doesn't like what you're doing, he'll "punish you." You're not always sure where the gray areas are, but you find out by the "wrath" or "boons" that "he" metes out to you. This kind of god is more like a devil. I believe God's truth here is that there are spiritual laws[79] that we keep or break. We set in motion our own effects. We experience pain from operating out of harmony with love until we have a change of heart, and a loving universe holds us.

We must do our part, get to know our light in Truth, own our dark energies and follow their teaching back to harmony. If we're willing to know ourselves fully, we won't have any trouble discerning whole truth from half-truth.

"Half a truth is often a great lie."

BENJAMIN FRANKLIN

---

77. See Format for Healing
78. See Glossary
79. See Spiritual Laws

EXISTENTIAL WOUNDS:

The existential wounds—those we all share—are a statement about the consciousness of humanity as a whole. We all have a common ground to some degree around survival, abandonment and worthiness. We've experienced according to our need and makeup the exact measure necessary for our healing. Comparison is non-applicable since we can't know what the other person has come in to do this time. So, as we step through our process from the highest place possible, we need to be in our intent to hold the other and ourselves in compassion, and in forgiveness.

Enough/Not Enough[80]

"There isn't enough, you have to grab what you need."

"You have to be on guard every moment because what you have can be taken away."

We're generally not aware of actually thinking these words, but they're present in our subtle emotions. These beliefs come from misconceptions in our deep psyche.

When we become aware of a continuing condition in our lives of not enough, we know that we hold a wrong belief about the true nature of Reality. The Truth is that there's *plenty* for everyone in this benign universe. So, if life seems to be stingy with us, it's our wrong belief that creates this reality. It's the energetic contraction of our demand (from our wounding) and the rage of the victim that keeps abundance at bay. The tight little ego is not open to the Divine flow; it wants what it wants for itself. It's disconnected from the web of light that joins us all and provides the free-flow of the energy of money, and all kinds of energy. .

The doubt as to whether or not there's enough for us to survive is a wound that we all carry to some extent. It's the existential wound of the 1st chakra[81] (at the perineum). The statement of the wound is something like, "I have *this* "meal, but I'm afraid the next one won't be

---

80. See Spiritual Laws, Law of Consciousness reflects Experience

81. See Additional Materials, Chakra Consciousness

there?" No amount of "meals" will satisfy this hole in our perception of life/God. We have to heal it from the inside out. But first, we have to come to terms with the fact that we have the misconception, and then go to our history to find the incarnational evidence of the wrong belief, and precisely how it came up this time.[82]

Perhaps we have plenty of the world's "stuff" but we keep peddling hard to get more and more so we can feel "full," so we can relax without fear—but we can never feel full or safe from this place.

It's necessary to know who we are and why we're here, to connect to the earth and all the beings on it and in it so that we can be—to use a popular word these days—sustainable in the way we live our lives. We need to know what's Real—that is, the energy and consciousness of my True Self; not my body, my lower mind connected to the mass consciousness, or my emotions caught in the past. We need to know what's important—purifying my lower energies, giving, and loving; not happiness for the separate small self, not money to make me feel good or to hoard, not being successful by the world's standards. The secret of abundance on planet earth is giving from the heart, "knowing" I already have everything, actually an embarrassment of riches. Gratitude becomes a way of life. It energetically opens us to guidance,[83] and calls the angels.

Abandonment/Constancy

Abandonment is the wound of the 2nd chakra (navel to pubic bone) that everybody shares, some more acutely than others, but we all "know" the fear of being left. We all guard, to some extent, against being left emotionally or physically. Out of these feelings sometimes we cling or pull energy, sometimes we demand, sometimes we leave first.

We have to do the work of our childhood wounding[84] in this regard. If we reach the place inside where we can bring the consciousness of our Godwoman that carries constancy, to the abandoned child, we

---

82. See Format for Healing
83. See Glossary
84. See Format for Healing

can bring light to where there is no light—we can heal the emotional attachment of the misconception.

When we articulate the misconception, we become aware that a shift begins, emotionally and energetically, away from the wrong belief to the Truth, even though the "emotional evidence," which is not reliable, would appear to support it. From the base of conscious and strong inner presence within ourselves, we weaken the emotional charge. When we occupy this state where we can hold multiple levels of consciousness, we're open to the Truth of omnipresence and can hold with compassion the soul's misconception that abandonment is part of the essence of God. This needs to be experienced as a palpable reality, not just a mental exercise. Through experiencing the feeling sense, we now know ourselves to have the capacity for constancy. *When we know it in ourselves, we can know it as present in the universe.*

Worthiness/Unworthiness

The existential wound of the third chakra (solar plexus) is unworthiness. We all carry that sense of not being enough, either consciously or unconsciously. For most of us, it shows up in certain situations and with certain people. We find ourselves in an uncomfortable emotional place and we try to blame ourselves out of it, push our way out of it, withdraw from it, etc. But, this place doesn't stay gone. It comes back again and again.

When we grab the thread of the unworthiness and follow where it leads, we find something in our childhood where we didn't measure up to someone's standards. The belief sounds something like, "I'm supposed to do better, be smarter, perform better." When we follow the thread, we find that we've internalized the childhood situation and don't accept or love ourselves—and consequently, others. It's not so much that the world finds us wanting, although we'll create that too, but that we project our belief onto the world. We need to work with this young and hurt part of us like the good parent, loving it back to loving itself.[85]

Deep within our psyche and deep within our emotions there's the knowledge that from our misconception, we step away from loving;

---

85. See Format for Healing

and close our hearts. Perhaps we show a loving mask to the world, perhaps we keep lots of "friends" around that don't really connect from the heart, perhaps we create lots of money and things to fill our life, but when we find the subtle emotional currents beneath, we see that there's a place where we let people get just so close and no closer. We "know" that the other doesn't accept us really, or won't when they get to know us better, and we're afraid we'll be destroyed if that person leaves us, or we're humiliated, or we're out of control in some way.

We undermine ourselves in life because we believe we're flawed, not entitled, and not capable of fulfilling our heart's desires. We distort our experience. We misconstrue everything around us. We're split-off from the best in us and look through the filter of "not good enough."

As we heal the "emotional truth," that is the misconception in the child and the soul, we can open to God's world. As we begin to deeply identify with the Truth that we are a piece of God and on a mission to heal ourselves and give to others, we find that "worthiness" has nothing to do with the true Reality. When we love to the best of our ability, we'll feel worthy.

We are love; there is nothing more to say.

"Everything is so dangerous that nothing is really very frightening."

GERTRUDE STEIN

DECISIONS/CHOICES

The idea is similar, but underneath the superficial layer, there's a world of difference between a decision and a choice. They're the same in that they both move energy into a certain direction. They're different in that the consciousness *behind* the movement is light years apart.

When we make a "decision," we add up the pluses and the minuses and go with whichever column has more weight. When we do this, we're giving up our ability to take a different path because of a list; a list arrived at by our limited perceptions of the moment.

When we make a choice, we look at the pluses and minuses and then take the path of our choosing. The minus list may be twice as long as the plus, and yet we may choose to take the direction of the minus side. When the choosing is healthy, we take full responsibility for it. If it doesn't turn out well, no person and no thing are blamed. This is the way of autonomy that is the master of thoughts and emotions. It's a state not at the affect of the world. It's taking responsibility for our choices. The choosing takes place from that inner, sacred place that is the heart of wisdom.

For example, when I was ready to help people, I thought about whether I should go to an accredited college and get a PhD, or whether I should study with a different kind of school. It took me several months of pondering the plusses and minuses of one approach over the other. I finally chose the "alternative" route to the mainstream. I was concerned that I might not find anything rigorous enough, or that would fit who I was; but I entered a program feeling the power and excitement of the choosing. I knew that if it went wrong, the buck stopped with me, and it felt good. (It didn't go wrong; it went very right. I chose to take a six-year program with the Pathwork. It turned out to be the best possible kind of PhD—deeply challenging inner work which laid the foundation to hold someone else from the heart of wisdom).

If you pull back from making a decision or a choice and let things ride, you are in fact making a choice. There is a wound behind the indecisiveness; it doesn't avoid difficulty, it makes more.

As we go deeper into spirit, we become aware that all choices boil down to either a choice for the light, the Truth of the heart, or a choice for the dark. This doesn't mean that we become a fanatic and see all of life in simplistic terms. It means that we take the path of the practical mystic and stay grounded as we soar into other realms. We see complexities that most people don't see. We're flexible because the Truth is flexible. We're aware of the part of us that is harmonized with God and the part that is not. We live most of the time from compassion, and we always ask ourselves: "Is this choice from love or fear?

"Life is either a daring adventure or nothing."

HELEN KELLER

POSITIVE PLEASURE/NEGATIVE PLEASURE

We've all heard of the sadist and masochist, usually associated with pain and sexuality. We think of negative pleasure mostly in this extreme. Negative pleasure is, in fact, an everyday occurrence. It happens below the level of our awareness, but if we're willing to look, we'll surely find it. It exists in those places where we experienced negativity in some form in our childhood and thought it was a reality of life.

The child attaches pleasure to its reality, whether positive or negative.

Pleasure is present in the childhood scenario because it's an intrinsic part of life energy. It's a part of all things good. It's our birthright. Life is supposed to be pleasurable. Relationships are supposed to be pleasurable. The experience of God is infused with pleasure. These may seem like simplistic statements, but when we feel into our deep emotions, we'll find that we believe otherwise, and that we're constantly searching for it.

As we look at our history, we may see that we've attached pleasure to being put down, to being loved but abused, to being criticized, etc. We get a sense of comfort from a familiar feeling from the past, and a feeling of rightness. We'll feel a strong pull, almost a compulsion, toward the negative person or situation that reminds us of the past.

The situation from our childhood may have been more indirect. Perhaps our mother tended to be aloof. Because we desperately wanted her love, we may now be drawn to aloof people, attaching pleasure and desirability to the aloofness. We may have been neglected and left alone a lot, so we attach the think/feel of lack of connection to a positive feeling in ourselves. Perhaps we weren't seen for whom we are, nothing we said had any merit, or we weren't understood; so we believe being safe is forcing others to pay attention to us—when we can do it, it feels good. Perhaps we knew we were loved, but didn't receive enough affection, so we might then feel pleasure in being loved and cared for.

As we grow up, these beliefs get pushed into the unconscious and we live them out. Because we attach pleasure to them, we enjoy feeling above everybody else, we enjoy being the powerful and omnipotent one, we enjoy being the one everybody loves. Pleasure gets attached to feeling superior, right, and from punishing those who are wrong and bad.

The negative pleasure has the characteristic of being like a "rush" from a drug. It peaks, feels good, and then goes away. We have to keep going after that rush again and again because this place can never be completely satisfied. It becomes a negative cycle in our lives. This is especially true about sexuality. We look for that "rush" in our sexual connection, which actually isn't connected at all. We try to squeeze our pleasure through a keyhole, instead of receiving pleasure by genuinely giving it.

When we make the connections and understand why we do these things, we shift dramatically. Our lives make sense. We know now a major piece of why we're stuck in certain behaviors. We have the motivation to withdraw energy from the negative pleasure. We can open to entraining with the vibratory level of the enduring, connected, deeply joyful and grateful experience of the Divine flow in this moment.

Positive pleasure is a thread in the tapestry of the universe. It's the smile of the Buddha.

> *"On the Sabbath try and make no noise that*
> *goes beyond your house.*
> *Cries of passion between lovers*
> *Are exempt."*

St. Thomas Aquinas

Virgin/Whore

This polarity has been around for a long, long time, and is the foundation of how women have been held for many centuries. It's prevalent even today in the emotional logic of people who think they have no prejudice.

The mainstream consciousness of our society sells things using women—and men, but mostly women—as objects. It's an animalistic approach to sexuality. The message is: "If you buy this car, you'll have lots of beautiful women to "shag." It's the human male animal's equivalent of the brightest plumage or the ability to kill off the competition, so they can get to put their penis into the vagina. This mentality holds the woman as the whore, to be used and discarded.

The virgin in the mass consciousness is the woman who has never had sex. She's to be revered for this. It's the common mistake of this mass consciousness idea that the man may revere the virgin, but he wants sex with a whore because she likes it. "We don't want to go to heaven because there is no sex in heaven!" It's surprising how many men and women believe these things under the level of their conscious mind. You have only to look at how "Madison Avenue" sexualizes everything. They're not doing this because they're immoral or bad people, objectified sex sells.

This attitude is extremely limited and unfulfilling. People are defined as a 2-dimensional "thing" rather than a full spectrum human being. We use them in a kind of masturbatory way—you have to look a certain way and touch certain places so I can climax. That's it. When we do connect with someone, we "fall in lust." We're isolated at the level of the 1st chakra[86] consciousness. There's no attempt to investigate the heart. The heart and the energies connected to it—kindness, goodness, love, and connectedness, to name a few—are disregarded and held separate. Sexuality has been cut off from love. This is one of our biggest splits. What the person does with their life, "who" they are, has little or no meaning. So when the time comes to work at relationship, we're out the door, mentally, emotionally or physically.

The real meaning of "virgin" is one who is pure of heart. We have to go to the third meaning in the dictionary under "whore" to find a non-sexual definition: debauch. Which means to corrupt morally, and when we think of morality we think of it most often as having a sexual connotation. It's telling in our society that we limit "virgin" and "whore" to sexual references.

We also name the worst insults possible in sexual terms. This is sexuality in the most disconnected sense. It's taking the most tender and intensely physical expression of love, making it dirty and using it to hurt.

Sometimes, the man is "stopped," actually stops himself, from

---

86. See Additional Materials, Chakra Consciousness

having sex with his wife because now they're married and she's the mother of his children. She's a virgin again—an emotional, non-articulated reality. She becomes the "Madonna." Also, women objectify men as caretakers and their relationships with their fathers limit full sexual expression with their mate. Women also collude with the mass consciousness by objectifying themselves.

As well as a thoughtform in the mass consciousness, the split between our genitals and our hearts is also present from our childhood wounding. So, as well as being conditioned from society, most of us have experienced a twisting of the sexual current in some way. This wounding can be physical, emotional, mental or spiritual. Nevertheless, the level doesn't matter—it's the issue itself that's primary. At the spiritual level, this is an issue with God. We've "forgotten" that the masculine and feminine are one. The feminine needs the masculine to take action; the masculine needs the feminine to be grounded. We've forgotten honoring, cherishing, loving. We all carry some of these mistaken ideas, denied intellectually, but carried out emotionally and through our actions.

Anything that separates is painful. Harmony, pleasure and peace come from integration and connectedness. Holding sex as separate from love is painful. Holding a person as an object for our own pleasure, or as a sexless, otherworldly untouchable is painful. We're animals and we need to have our animal nature fully, but we're not *only* animals. We're spirit also. To be healthy, we must inhabit our bodies and because we're more, we must integrate spirit, mind, and emotions *with* the body. Spirit needs to come down through the levels and through the physical for us and for the other. If the body is in service to the heart, we move into bliss.

The experience of "making love" and being present with someone you respect, honor and love, is ecstatic. The sexual act moves from using the other's body to stimulate for orgasm, to letting go of the compulsion for "the peak experience" and bringing focus to pleasuring the beloved. A dynamic and enduring vortex of pleasure and love is created. Through the focus on giving, we discover the secret of continual pleasure, on all levels. This is a different world. This is a world where we let go of any agenda, where we can relax, where we create heightened sensitivity and total fulfillment.

It's time for the concepts of "virgin" and "whore" that we carry in little, closed-off pockets of our being to disappear into cherishing every human being.

> *"Know the true nature of your Beloved.*
> *In His loving eyes your every thought, word,*
> *and movement is always, always*
> *beautiful."*

HAFIZ

NAMING/LABELING

Are we supposed to know what's happening before our eyes? Often, we won't let ourselves know what we see, hear and feel. We don't want to deal with unpleasant things. We don't want to put someone into a box. Or we do. In which case, we label them. Sometimes, if we don't say it out loud, we're yelling it in our heads…"asshole," "insensitive slob," "bastard," "bitch," and on and on. We know we shouldn't. So, we may ricochet to the other end of the pole and refuse to "see" anything negative—we become a kind of "Pollyanna." We don't know what's right. Our emotions are straining toward reaction into judgment[87] or criticism. Perhaps our idealized sense of ourselves says that we *should* "appear" kind and loving. If we can witness a deeper part of ourselves, however, we discover that our heart *wants* to love. Both of the extremes have a piece of the heart's Truth. People do act out in negative ways, and everyone has a Divine Spark.

When we wake up to the places where we're reactive and in denial, we can then inhabit that deep witness of our hearts and "name" the thing it's *right* name, which is discerning what is without judgment or charge. We can make an observation such as: "this person is acting out their negativity by attempting to put me down." Or, "I just let my anger fly with my four-year-old grandson." When I can name the energy from deep Truth, I can deal with it in the other or myself from compassion. I can make amends to the one I've hurt, and per-

---

87. See Glossary

haps name the energy to the person[88] who wanted to put me down. If that person won't hear you or goes into emotional reaction, it can be best to go straight to forgiveness.

In our own inner process, when we give an energy its right name, it begins to dissolve. We've brought God's Truth to it, and the tightness inside relaxes into compassion.

If we try to whitewash it, rationalize it, or excuse it, we're not in Truth. When we can name it it's right name, we're loving ourselves, we're letting go of unconscious guilt for dishonesty and we inhabit a strength and integrity that no one and nothing can shake.

When we bring understanding and compassion to our thoughts about others, and ourselves we practice mastery of the mind and reveal the unconscious negative impulses so they can be transformed.

> *"...As each soul nears heaven differences will dissolve to such*
> *a sublime extent that when the heart looks upon*
> *any object in this world it*
> *will cry "Beloved."*

St. John of the Cross

TALKING/LISTENING

Most of us don't give much thought to what we say, or for that matter what other people say.

Even those of us who've looked inside ourselves, often don't listen to our own words. We don't think about what we say. We often say what the other person wants to hear. We say things to "give an impression." We interrupt. Some of us talk incessantly, and some of us have difficulty expressing ourselves. Our 5th Chakra[89] is out of balance.

We're imbalanced because we weren't allowed to speak our minds or stand up for ourselves. We "swallowed" our authentic self and negativities that overpowered us.

We carry wounds around not being heard, seen and understood

---

88. See Glossary, Confrontation
89. See Additional Materials, Chakra Consciousness

which can cause us to override someone else's expression or be so anxious to be heard that we ignore whom the other person is and what they want to communicate. We use them for a sounding board. This, of course, produces what we least want. The person we're talking "at" feels unseen or unheard and will turn off and withdraw from interaction with us. We need to pay attention to our speech and listening habits and find out what we're doing, or not doing. Then, we track back from our behavior to the wound.[90]

Have you had the exquisite experience of someone deeply listening to you? Where you know they're not thinking of what to say, or of something else, or getting distracted. They're empty except for taking you in. If you've experienced it, you now it's an incredible gift. It heals that tender place that isn't sure we exist.

As we learn more about ourselves and purify, we can witness the agendas of our personality[91] when we're interacting. We begin to cultivate the objectivity and positive will to hold the false needs of our wounding and bring our intent to being present and connected. We focus more on the process, less on the end product. We aren't interested in "fixing" someone, or attached to any "forcing current."[92] We're present to the inner spaciousness where all is well, and we hold a "good opinion" of the other. We're connected to the deep ocean of peace and love and transmit[93] this energy as we interact. We've discovered the power of the word.

We wake up to being conscious to the moment and present in our bodies when we speak and when we listen. We hold the intention to be in integrity with the Truth of God, not the truth of our anger, opinions or judgments; and to speak and listen from the Heart.

We become the balanced expression through the throat chakra of love and Truth. We're surrendered to God's will, which is the will of our deepest hearts longing.

Every word and every silence says, "I love you."

---

90. See Format for Healing
91. See Glossary
92. Ibid
93. Ibid

"I have listened to the realm of the Spirit.
I have heard my own soul's voice,
and I have remembered that love
is the complete and unifying
thread of existence."

MARY CASEY

"Our lives begin to end the day we become silent
about things that matter."

MARTIN LUTHER KING

LEADER/FOLLOWER

In the mass consciousness, the attitude prevails that it's good to be a leader and it's second-rate to follow. This logic says that if you're a follower, you must strive to be the leader because that's all that counts. Being the leader means, to most people, having power *over* others. This is the mark of success.

The downside of this philosophy is that you're never satisfied with where you are, and are always pitted against everyone else to get to the top. When we do get to the top, there are all those others out there that want to rip you down from your pedestal and take your place. Not only are those "under" you trying to unseat you, but also they resent your egotistical lordliness, verbalized or not.

The unhealed ego wants to have power over, but doesn't want to carry the responsibility to the task, and especially not to the troops. This kind of leader is always watching their back and interested mostly in the gratification of the "small self" (the unhealed ego). Whether or not this kind of leader knows it, she is taking the negative energy from the followers—the other half of the negative circle of giving it.

First, let's back up and perceive this "being the leader" from a different perspective. Let's unhook from the mass consciousness and consider the attributes of what a real leader should have. There is a completeness and autonomy necessary to step up and take responsibility for a task. This completeness presupposes that this person "knows the ropes," that is, has been able to follow a leader, without rancor, be a team player, and learn. If we try to lead without this foundation, we'll have a sense of being a fake—and, we are a fake! We'll spend most of our time trying to prove that we have the power.

If we follow from a place of envying the leader, we're contracted and self-involved. When we can be both a follower and a leader from the best in us, we're able to allow a life process that shifts and changes as circumstances dictate—like the geese that continually change positions in their V-formation, with each taking a turn at the lead. From this place, we can hold the energies of leading and following as fluid positions that we have the capacity to move in and out of as needed. If we think of following as a task that we bring our attention and presence to with the intention of supporting the leader in the best way we're capable, then there's no judgment and no reaction to following.

True leadership comes from an intention to give. It's a place that's willing to take feedback, holds an objective state, and will admit when impartiality has been compromised. It's willing to put aside the petty little ego and put the task at hand first. It contains a power sourced in love. It can contain[94] negative emotions and thoughts about the other. It's willing and able to tolerate frustration[95] and the slings and arrows that invariably get hurled at leaders. The mature leader will also take the transference[96] present in the group. Transference comes from the "wounded child" that envies, but doesn't want to take the responsibility that comes with true leadership; this "child" wants it's own god biased in their favor; and wants someone else to run their lives, but resents them for it.

Out of this wounding comes our issues with authority in general that must be looked at if we're to be a strong leader and a balanced follower. As children we submitted, fought against, or withdrew from the authority of our parents. This place is filled with unresolved issues and deep emotion. We transfer our unresolved issues onto any and all authority figures.

---

94. See Glossary

95. Ibid

96. See Transference/True Love; Additional Materials, Transference/Counter-Transference

On the spiritual level, the issues with our parents are mirrors of our soul misconceptions about the nature of the Godforce. We have to do our inner work so that our discernment and our ability to center in our Godwoman/man are not clouded.

The mature leader carries an *inner* authority. This means that there is an ability to connect with a place inside that is the Loving Witness[97] and sits in compassionate attention to the inner and outer workings of one's world. It carries it's own knowing. It witnesses every thought, emotion, word, outer circumstance and lets the wisdom of the heart decide where energy will be put and where it will be withheld. This is the authentic self (the ego connected and harmonized with the Divine) that is aware of it's weaknesses and it's strengths, is in touch with a wide spectrum of feelings, has the ability to "get bigger" until equanimity is reached, can hold the tension of opposites— both inner and outer—and can respond[98] rather than react.[99] Inner authority has a direct connection to God. It doesn't *say*, however, that it hears the words of God and you don't. That would be a misuse of power. In the case of true inner authority, the Truth comes through the vehicle with humility.

The following is true of all good leaders, I believe, and an especially important touchstone for spiritual groups:

"True spiritual leaders will not try to hold you in subordinate patterns, but will pull you, as quickly as they can, to their own level, and push you, if you are capable of going, beyond."[100]

> *"The words Guru, Swami, Super Swami, Master, Teacher, Murshid, Yogi, Priest,*
> *Most of those sporting such a title are*
> *Just peacocks.*

> *The litmus test is:*

---

97. See Glossary
98. Ibid
99. Ibid
100. Kenneth X. Carey, Raphael, <u>The Starseed Transmissions,</u> 2nd Printing (San Francisco: HarperSanFrancisco, 1984), 62.

Hold them upside down over a cliff for a few hours.
If they don't wet their pants
Maybe you found a real one.

KABIR

LIVING/DYING

To live is to die, and to die is to live.

That's a cryptic statement; so let me explain.

If we really want to live to the fullest, it's necessary for the ego to die to our old habits, our cherished ways of being and thinking, our fears. That is, we have to take our fear by the hand and jump off "the cliff" of our comfort zone.

There's a thought/feel in our wounded ego that believes certain things are "death": "If I make a mistake, I won't be loved and therefore I'll die," "If I don't work all the time, I won't get enough money and I'll die," "If I don't submit, I'll be abandoned and I'll die," "If I feel my pain, I'll die," "If I feel helplessness, I'll die." We, of course, don't articulate these fears, but they run our lives from the "invisible cockpit" in our deep psyche.

Life *seems* safe by holding on tightly and somehow making it through with as little difficulty as possible. Although, the truth is we have lots of difficulty anyway. This tight, defensive position cuts off our feelings so our life experience is limited, at best. When we really live, we walk *toward* difficulty. We turn to face our fears. That's what everything boils down to, a deep split: love or fear. Where there's fear, there's no love.

Once we decide to let go of the tight grip we have on ourselves, we awaken to deeper inner dimensions. We become accustomed to peeling our fingers off the lifeline we've been clutching for "safety"—which really is attached to nothing!—and be different from the rest (or, if we spend our lives being different, to be ordinary!).

Once we start "dying," we'll die on all levels—mental, emotional, physical, and even spiritual. On the spiritual level, we need to die to our wrong beliefs about God—for instance, "the universe provides, but it doesn't love." "The world is loving, but it doesn't back you up."

These beliefs aren't conscious, but they show up in the patterns and emotional currents of our lives.

The emotional level is the most difficult for most of us. It's so strong that we believe our emotional reactions and negative feelings are real. For most, it defines reality: "If I feel it, it's what's so, this emotion is me and I must react from it."

We fear our darkness. The unhealed ego has to "die" to it—that is, let go of the ideas we cling to about whom we are, and accept Reality.

The part of us that's in denial has to "die" to acceptance of our physical death. We're afraid of physical death because we're afraid of the unknown—the unknown consisting of anything we're not familiar with from our personality—the "small self." So this limited "self" clings to its safe little box, and pushes away anything that hints at change. This clinging contracts our mind, emotions and body—our energy, and we never live and love fully.

If not consciously, then certainly unconsciously, we know our limitations and faults, our negativities, and may look upon death as the final payback—our annihilation.

A part of the unknown that we fear is our unconscious (both positive and negative), and letting go of control, as in "falling" deeply in love with someone. Living fully requires that we take chances, look like a fool, love like a fanatic! The dictionary says a fanatic is someone whose beliefs take them out of reality. Yes, yes, yes, that's it exactly!! Our reason is compromised by the limitation of our conditioning and tight holding against life. Our reason needs to "die" into our Wisdom.

The Reality of physical death is that it's the movement from one dimension to another. The physical shell dissolves back to the earth and our spiritual "self," our consciousness, moves to the next level. When we recognize ourselves as a part of "source," "God," "the force," we know that we can never "disappear." Not only can't we disappear, but also we're needed to take our place with the forces of light.

When we open to the Reality that we can leave the physical body at any time, and that we may need illness or injury for evolvement, we enter the Reality of the moment. If we accept life as it is, we'll begin to live with passion, excitement and groundedness, as if we might die in the next moment—which we might! If we live accepting this Truth of life, we live to the fullest possible extent.

> Death... "It is a mystery of paramount impact. Death helps us explain the meaning of what we do in our lives. Its finality places our intentions, our thoughts, and our deeds in context. If we reflect on it thoroughly, the significance of each moment becomes known. We can choose to live in a shallow manner. We can choose to live deeply with sincerity of purpose. We can choose to follow mind and desire; we can choose to affirm God's presence through compassion, love, kindness, patience, and justice. When the profound value of each moment is measured we can say "yes" to life, affirming God's gift with our entire being. A heart complete with such gratitude can receive the wisdom that penetrates the veils of mystery."
>
> M.R. Bawa Muhaiyaddeen[101]

Blessings/Curses

No, we haven't transported to the middle Ages! While the energies were quite a bit denser on the planet then, people were also more open to the reality of realms that we cannot see.

Blessings and curses have validity—they are ways to use energy.[102] Our thoughts, words and deeds send energy to specific people, and into the universe. What we send out is subject to the law of cause and effect.[103] We're responsible for our energy whether we're aware of it or not.

Blessings and curses are simply positive and negative energy that it's possible to "send" to someone, or to ourselves. We do it all the time, mostly unaware. On the negative side, we may initiate the energy by saying, "Whenever there's a bug, I catch it," or "Over my dead

---

101. M.R. Bawa Muhaiyaddeen, *To Die Before, Death, The Sufi Way of Life* (Philadelphia: The Fellowship Press, 1997, XI.

102. See Approaching Healing Energetically

103. See Spiritual Laws

body!" Or we may say something like, "I can never make ends meet," or "You will always be second rate!" Blessings may look like, "Happy Birthday to you…and many more!" or "Be Well," or "Good Morning!" or "God Bless you!"

We don't think about what we're saying or that we're sending or calling in energy. We say oaths and pledges mindlessly. We don't realize the impact of our words, emotions, or thoughts—or someone else's. Negative energy sent to you may hurt your feelings and then be forgotten, but if it happens to hit a wound, you may hold onto it for years or for your whole life…perhaps lifetimes. In such a case, it will add to the thoughtforms you already carry in conjunction with your wound; and it will add "juice" to the negative emotions that are connected with it.

In the case of curses, we must become aware of the negativity we carry. We need to ask ourselves questions and be willing to answer them honestly, such as, "Where have I sent negativity to another?" Where in me is there a receptor site for receiving negative energy?" When we've sent negativity to another, in order to ameliorate the energy, we must see the error of our ways, the misconception that sent the energy, and bring in the healed paradigm. That is, we need to recognize and feel the negative energy, understand how we came by it,[104] and find the truth of the matter. If we've sent a "curse" to someone, we must revoke it, then connect with our love to the highest degree possible for the other and ourselves.

As we're more aware of these energies and their power, we can bring in our positive intent and our positive will to live the life of Blessings. That is, while we continue to purify our darkness, we can use the negative discoveries as an impetus to turn our focus to blessing everyone and everything as we walk through our day. The Buddhists use this practice a lot, and it's very beautiful. They'll often say things like, "May all beings reach enlightenment," "May all beings be happy."

I'm aware as I'm writing and sitting here getting my hair done that I'm wanting to connect with my stylist—she's a very special person. She's preoccupied. I'm unhappy about that and find myself

---

104. See Format for Healing

falling into critical thoughts about her. I become aware of what I'm doing. I consciously turn to my heart looking for the love, and send her a blessing…"May you have joy in your heart today." I hold her in good will. A wave of joy brushes my heart.

When done with sincerity, shifting your energy into a higher vibration is a deep prayer.

"There are beautiful wild forces within us.
Let them turn the mills inside
and fill
sacks
that feed even heaven.

ST. FRANCIS OF ASSISI

HEALTH/ILLNESS

Health doesn't have so much to do with the body. Health comes from a deeper level of our being than the outer shell.

The body is the outer manifestation of our genes and also our thoughts and emotions, and at the deepest level the state of our soul. We use the genes we were born with and shape the body from our thoughts and emotions, our wounding and our harmony. We work with the qualities we've been given and what comes to us in life. We make choices on how we use our energy, to support health on all levels or not. The level beneath this field of play is the soul and it's task for this lifetime. This is the source that stimulates the choices that create the outer manifestation of the body and the person we are.

It's not necessarily true that the healthiest body reflects the healthiest soul. The soul uses the body for many purposes. A soul may incarnate to learn certain lessons through physical illness and be a very advanced soul. Or, a soul may incarnate to die at birth or as a child to pay off a karmic debt or to bring a teaching to the parents. Depending upon the state and manner of the soul's path, the body may show a manifestation of the harmony of our mind and emotions, or it may be the ground through which we learn and our consciousness grows.

So, it could be the case that our greatest growth could be to die of a disease. We can, therefore, never compare ourselves to anyone else.

We have to take these factors into consideration when someone we know and love is ill or has been injured. Is it really in their highest good to live? Is it in their highest good to fight from the personality when the Higher Self has chosen to die? It's hard to be sure, but if we're asking these questions, we're on the right track. Sometimes what's needed at the soul level is for the person to fight for themselves and their life, and sometimes not.

The more we can embrace an expanded consciousness in holding our body, the more sense everything makes and the more we find peace in our heart. Our body is borrowed from the earth. It is truly a temple for a piece of God.

> *"A chalice—the Grail—my body became, for it held the Christ and He drank*
> *from me."*

ST. TERESA OF AVILA

TRANSFERENCE/TRUE LOVE

Well, first, "What *is* "transference?" and then, "What does that have to do with true love?"

When you use your "x-ray vision" and look deep into a relationship, you see that these two things are intimately related. Transference, at the deepest level, is the misconceptions about God/the universe/the all, that we "transfer" onto our parents. We come into the incarnation wanting to heal places in our soul that have forgotten that the universe is benign and caring, rational and balanced, a place where everything is connected and where nothing dies, but only changes form.

Our parents ignite these misconceptions in us in a spectrum of ways, from very gently to very strongly—whatever our soul needs. This "igniting" takes the form of emotional wounding, so we can experience the misconception in the deepest way, feeling. We get wounded with concepts like, "all men are brutal," "all women are cheats," "everyone is out to get me," "I don't have what it takes," "There's not enough," " I'll be abandoned," "I'm not loved," "sex is dirty." We then cope with the wounding by developing a defense: I'll withdraw, aggress, or submit. Now, we push all this into our unconscious, grow up and find a relationship. Uh, oh. We're in trouble!

We don't know that we're "protecting" ourselves with a defense, or that we're transferring onto (pasting on) our beloved the unresolved issues with our parents. We don't see our partner clearly, we're seeing and experiencing through the distorted lens of our wounding and defense. We might have emotional beliefs like, "You're a wonderful man, but I'm watching you closely because I know you'll leave me." What happens when we hold the vibration, thoughts and feelings of this misconception is that we may evoke that energy from the other, see it where it's not—or, actually draw someone who will leave us. Then, the child in us has *proved* what it "knew" all along!

The force of the transference is a mighty thing. It's amazing any relationship survives! And, the truth is that most relationships are not healthy. People either divorce, have another life within the marriage—affairs, work, a consuming hobby, or form an armed camp. In an armed camp, each person digs in with their "rightness," keeps up appearances and holds the other at an emotional distance. Sometimes, the neuroses match, like the woman who never had a father and the husband who needs to be a father.

Most often, we're attracted to someone because they exhibit characteristics that we experienced in our parents, and the opposite. For instance, if one of our parents were criticizing and fault finding, we would probably be "turned on" by someone who was cruel in this way because the child in us would feel a compulsive draw to the familiar and "comfortable," and be striving to finally get that elusive parent to treat them well and love them. Once we're in the relationship, we realize we can't change our partner and we become brutalized, again. Our heart "shrinks back" from the pain of it. Or, we might go into denial, align with the aggressor and aggrandize our partner's "savvy" or quick wit. We've turned away from ourselves, from our beauty and light.

There's another factor from our history that influences who we're drawn to.

It's a truth that there was one parent that we felt more loved by than the other. The parent we felt "less loved by" holds the characteristics we will always be drawn to. For instance, perhaps the parent we felt less loved by was aloof. Therefore, we'll always find aloofness attractive because our child was on a quest to get more love from that parent.

There are other factors, also, like being drawn to someone who has something we feel we don't or being drawn to someone who treats us like royalty when we feel like we're nothing.

The point is we're attracted to someone very, very often as an automatic reaction to our history. It always works out on the deep level of our healing, however, because we keep having the negative relationships so we can get the teaching. However, when we're ready, we want to do the healing work and know a healthy, loving relationship when it comes to us. Or, perhaps, recognize we *have* a loving relationship but we've been blind to it.

So, how do we begin to know what true love is, when we know transference is present? A partial answer is that transference is always present. We don't have to be totally healed of it, we just need to know the territory. If I know I have a tendency to be drawn to brutal men or dictatorial women, I can take a look at who I'm with and check it out. I can ask myself sincere and honest questions, or get help from someone a little ahead of me on the path. I can follow my emotional reactions to my childhood wounds. Once the child is found,[105] we can begin to relax the death-grip we have on our wild emotions and they're corresponding mental litany. We can recognize what's happening, and thereby teach ourselves to look for our adult—our God-woman/Godman,[106] the peace of home base.

So, in relationship with a beloved, when something goes wrong and we have an emotional reaction,[107] that's our signal that we're in the past. We need to take a break and go inside. When we've found the wound and worked on bringing love and understanding to the part of us that's still in the pain of separation and emotional charge, we can then turn to the "issue" with the other and own 110% of the cause. (Even though it may feel like it's 98% the other's "fault," this

---

105. See Format for Healing
106. See Glossary
107. Ibid

is not in reality). The presence of an emotional reaction is a sure sign that we've taken the present and made it the past, and consequently, that our perception is skewed.

If there were no holdovers from the past, and someone said or did something hurtful, we would simply raise our eyebrows in surprise or smile—and ask ourselves, "What did I do or think or feel to invite this?" This is not a mea culpa, a neurotic "I'm *always* at fault for *everything*," but rather it's the expansion of consciousness beyond the personality.

We must go to the heart consciousness. The most important thing in our interactions is to do our inner work. We have to turn around from straining outward to face ourselves. This is a place where we are at choice point. Do we listen to the voice of limitation, or do we grow? This is how relationship can help us to unhook from our negative tendencies, to become more loving.

There's a point at which you can hold yourself and the other with the defenses *and* the love. You're more in balance. And, when you're in balance, you know that what matters most is not the love you get, but the love you give.

This is the path to true love.

> *"Does God only pucker at certain moments*
> *of one's life?*
> *No way!*
> *He is the wildest of us*
> *Lovers."*

HAFIZ

SOME MISCONCEPTIONS ABOUT LIFE/SOME TRUTHS ABOUT LIFE

Some Misconceptions About Life:
- Either—Or, I'm either totally happy or totally in pain
- I'm not supposed to get hurt
- Self-effacement is a virtue
- I'm either good *or* bad

- I am making choices
- The body is not holy
- If I don't punish, it won't get done
- I do things for reasons
- My way is the right and true way
- If you hurt me, I have the right to hurt you back
- Darkness is outside of God
- I am my body, my mind, my emotions

Some Truths About Life:

- The "other" is innocent to our wounds
- Energy follows thought
- Pain is a part of life and its role is to teach me
- I have a number of "subpersonalities" (often archetypes) and a Real Self that is an adult connected to spirit
- We create our lives
- In the last analysis, we do things because we are choosing either the light or the dark
- Our goal in life is to love more
- We have to do the work
- We never act out on anyone
- We want what we fear the most
- We walk to God from the spine and bow, not from the infant that begs
- We are a part of God and are *needed* in the web of interconnectedness of all things

Section 3 – Integration

GOD'S TRUTH/EGO'S TRUTH

When we start paying attention to the Reality under the surface of things, we become tuned in to the workings of our mind and emotions, and our capacity to discern becomes more reflective and connected to a deeper well of objectivity and Wisdom.

As we become a more acute witness to ourselves, we notice that there are disparate "voices" in our heads. Some are harmonious and some not. This is not pathology, but a Reality that has been on the edge of our awareness. We're all familiar with thoughts that say, "I want that donut," and another thought that says, "Don't have it, it'll make you fat." But we seldom stop and think about what is actually happening.

The disharmonic "voices" we carry come from the unhealed ego. These are the source of the "ego's truth." They represent split-off parts of ourselves and are often akin to the archetypes.[108] Since our split-off parts are not harmonic, they cause pain. Once we become aware and can name these energies, we can discern "who" is speaking. Intrinsic in making this determination is the embodiment of the Witness, which directs the healing and integration.

"God's Truth" is the Truth of Love that comes through the Witness. God's Reality transcends the material world. It discerns all— light and dark—and holds it in compassion. God's Truth is flexible, inclusive and never hurts.

An example of finding and naming these energies may be a situation where a person wants to belittle you. Your "ego's truth" may be that the person is an "asshole," "stupid," "misguided," or "evil," depending upon your orientation. But, the bottom line is that there will be a value judgment and a "make wrong." "God's Truth" may be that

---

108. See Glossary

the "belittler" feels inferior and unhappy. (This could be a defensive posture to cope with a cruel parent). It may also be True that *your* child was belittled and needs to know that he is good enough. When you bring in another level of healing to your wound, and connect with your Loving Witness, you can let go of the "ego's truth" and drop into a deeper space with more perspective and come to, "oh, yes, I understand." This is not a mentalized understanding, but rather a full-body understanding—mental, emotional, physical, and spiritual. You could say that "God's Truth" here is that the both of you were drawn together by like vibrations to heal another layer.

Through the search for wisdom and love within our own hearts, and the willingness to let go of our negative impulses to "make bad and wrong," we gradually bring in the realization of what's True. We know it because we feel it, and feelings are the river that carries us to God.

> *Mother Teresa says she sees*
> *"the face of Christ in all his distressing disguises."*

ACTIVE/BEING

Active/Passive, Male/Female, Aggressor/Victim—there are many nuances of meaning as we explore the active state and the being state. When we look at the active and being states exemplified by male and female, we're led into a labyrinth. In our society, there is still a great deal of misconception about what exactly is male and what's female. The male characteristics and roles of provider, protector, intellectual, leader, worth more, not emotional, and stud are generally accepted as being masculine (active). The female characteristics and roles of nurturer, dependent, weak, stupid, emotional, and sex object are generally accepted as being feminine (passive). Even though we may consider ourselves to be enlightened in this respect, there are still places in our unconscious and emotions that "accept" these roles as truth. We may even be in reaction to them, which is still deeply enmeshed with the misconception.

As well as being born into a gender, we also each carry within both masculine and feminine. A man may carry a mostly feminine state of being, while a woman may carry mostly a masculine state of being. So, as we look at healing the energies, we must look at both in ourselves.

As we make an attempt to peel away the cultural roles from the basic energy of the active and being states, we find something very different from the mass consciousness. It's more easily understood, I think, if we call the energies active and being because masculine and feminine carry so many associations.

Active and being are two energies that cannot exist without each other. *Each carries the other within.*

The active energy sits inside the being, ready to move for an efficient and appropriate period that is precisely calibrated to what is needed to complete the action. Its meaningful and relaxed action, and carries the energies of the protector, definer, speaker, and giver. When the active moves, it carries within it the beingness. If you watch a rushing stream, and look and feel into it, you'll find the beingness within the moving water.

The being state holds the active within. It's alive, awake, and present. It's the holder of energy—the void; it's listening and receiving. It's the involuntary, allowing, trustful waiting, meaning, letting it be, letting it ripen, soft, readiness, waiting to unfold.

So, while we must let go of our conditioning and mind-set about feminine and masculine, we also need to heal. In general terms, the historical masculine needs to heal his brutality. He needs to drop the armor over his heart, to soften, and allow his tenderness. Again, in general terms, the historical feminine needs to take self-responsibility. She has been losing herself by surrendering to the active principle of another instead of her own. She submits and lives off the man; she's fearful of the man, of life; and makes herself a slave. Often, when healing the twist in their masculine energy, the man will fall into the twisted feminine—lose autonomy, become dependent. And, the woman will often hit the pole of the twisted masculine in her desire to come into balance. I remember when I divorced at 35 with two children, I was so afraid that I couldn't make my way in the world that I automatically took on the attitude of the emotionally cut-off "dragon slayer."

The twist in the masculine can be healed by an intent to open the heart and emotional body. The twist in the feminine can be healed by a willingness to be accountable, and an intent to be strong and in life. Both need to go inside for their answers and not blame the other.

In addition to healing where there may be a twist in our masculine and feminine, we also want to hold the intention to balance the active and being states. When we're in active mode, we so often pull our energies out in front of our bodies, straining and forcing. When we're in the being mode, we often leave our bodies energetically and become stagnant. Working on the balance is a spiritual practice where we pay attention to how we're using our energy. In a relaxed way, we can observe ourselves and do the fine-tuning. We can hold as a mentor the rushing stream—how wonderful the feeling of doing a task from the quietness within. Actually, when we slow down, we go faster.

> *"Once a group of thieves stole a rare diamond larger than two*
> *goose eggs.*
> *Its value could have easily bought three thousand horses and three*
> *thousand acres of the most fertile land in Shiraz.*
> *The thieves got drunk that night to celebrate their great haul,*
> *but during the course of the evening the effects of the liquor,*
> *and their mistrust of each other grew to such an extent*
> *they decided to divide the stone into pieces.*
> *Of course then the Priceless became lost.*
> *Most everyone is lousy at math and does that to God –*
> *dissects the Indivisible One,*
> *by thinking, by saying,*
> *"This is my Beloved, he looks like this and acts like that,*
> *how could that moron over there*
> *really be*
> *God?"*

Hafiz

MAKERS/DESTROYERS

If we look at these words for a while and let ourselves drop inside, we discover that we really know all about this. Which one am I? Or, which one am I sometimes? Could it be possible that I carry a belief, manifesting overtly or covertly, that I should undo, undermine, separate? Do I also carry a belief in harmony and positive creation? How do I manifest these tendencies?

The energy of building or enhancing self and other may be felt, but is not usually acknowledged in our society. To build up for it's own sake is seen as weakness in our "cut-throat" business world, and that attitude is accepted as a social norm. Someone is "savvy" if they're suspicious, critical and are always on the lookout for an opportunity to put someone down. Often they're verbally adept. They can even make us—and others—laugh while they're making us stupid, clumsy or wrong. Actually, if you react to the "slap", you're ridiculed as "too sensitive;" "can't take a joke." Recognize that? Yes, most of us do.

What we don't do is call it by its right name—negative/dark/tearing down/destroying. It's a way that the darkness sneaks through us and passes as acceptable behavior. The darkness likes to hide in plain sight. While we refuse to acknowledge it, it has lots of influence and runs rampant through us. So, we want to ask ourselves the question, "How do I run negative energy that I rationalize?" "Is my negative ego getting a rush from putting others down?

Talking negatively about someone behind her back is another way darkness hides in plain sight. This is maligning, energetically putting a knife in someone's back. The energy of the "word" goes to them and affects them. This is also considered "socially acceptable." We have "fun" talking about the "geek" or the "one with a card short of a whole deck."

We also destroy our bodies. We go with our desires and put in it things that don't build health. Why do we do this? It doesn't make any sense logically. It does make emotional sense, however. We do it because we want to soothe ourselves; because we want to protect ourselves; because we were hungry as a child; because we're tired, angry, upset; because we want to indulge ourselves; because we hate ourselves. We "forget" that the body is a gift, a vehicle that we use so we can affect matter and learn the deep truths of the universe. It's a sacred thing.

There's a place in the consciousness of men and women where we're numb to defilement. We defile the innocent. We do this physically, mentally, emotionally and spiritually—men with women; women with men; adults with children, humans with animals, plants, and the earth. Where do I close my heart and participate in this?

When we look a little beneath the surface, we find that we're all destroyers in some way. This needs to be acknowledged and deeply felt before we can, in reality, hold the positive pole.

To "make" is to be aware of the preciousness of life. It's the energy embodied that wants to love and serve. It's the part of us that sees and acknowledges the beauty in people—the world, the universe, and ourselves. It's the energy that will hold someone with the heart that is stumbling in some way, or even someone who's acting out negatively. This consciousness recognizes that we're all the same. It knows that the duality is just our teacher. It's the consciousness that everything and everyone is holy. It's the knowledge that we're the builders, the ones who reveal the connectedness of all beings and all things.

We're all makers, too.

We need to find it and embody it.

Our "maker" needs to heal our destroyer.

This is a level beneath our defenses and wounding, and beneath our excuses and rationalizations.

It's the level of intention.

"Can true humility and compassion exist in our words and eyes
unless we know we too are capable of
any act?"

                                        ST. FRANCIS OF ASSISI

INDIVIDUALITY/UNITY

When we embark on a spiritual path, and we hit our striving for the realization of God, we find a conflict in our ego. There is the part of the ego that is aligned with harmony which wants to surrender to the Truth and the Love; and, there's a part in us that holds onto our 'individuality" and doesn't want to lose it. What we generally think of as our "individuality" actually amounts to separateness (pride, superiority, selfishness, fear) and comes from the "little ego,"[109] the unhealed aspect of the personality. The "little ego" is terrified of losing its independence, that is, what it identifies as the separate "me." It represents the part of us that's frightened and contracted. It's the consciousness of disconnectedness from others, the earth, and the universe. It clings to the status quo and what it can control, and thus denies the realities of change, other realms and death. It isn't in the scope of its understanding or interest to think of itself as limitless, loving unconditionally, connected, letting go, or selfless.

We must be healed and harmonized to a certain critical mass in order for the vessel (the self)[110] to handle the high vibration of God's love and truth. We enter the high vibrations—Christ Consciousness[111]—gradually, adjusting as we go. To the extent there are still places we will not look, where we will not know our lower self, to that extent the vessel is impure, and to that extent we are separate, alone and "individual."

The small part of us thinks that by surrendering to the merging with another human being—that is, God, that we'll lose our individuality and our consciousness will be obliterated.

What we discover as we heal the cut-off, wounded parts of the ego is that there is a piece of truth in the concept of our "individuality," and that is our uniqueness. We each carry a particular mixture of the qualities[112] of God that no other being has. Our unique energy is needed to complete the universe.

The more we open the uniqueness of our "true selves," the more conscious we become and the further we move into the unitive[113] state. We keep our consciousness as we merge, as we do when we melt into bliss. But this is a deep consciousness, the knowing without judgment

---

109. See Glossary

110. Ibid

111. Ibid

112. Ibid

113. Ibid

and the recognition of heaven on earth, not the machinations of the lower mind. The lower mind gets transformed and merged with the greater consciousness of love, as are the parts of us now that are harmonized. The split-off, contracted and lonely "individual" finally finds what it has been looking for all along—itself as love.

> *"God revealed a sublime truth to the world*
> *when He sang, "I am made whole by your life,*
> *Each soul,*
> *Each soul completes me."*

HAFIZ

FORCES OF LIGHT/FORCES OF DARKNESS

As we look at the forces of Light and darkness, we want to pay special attention to centering in our Light. It's a common misconception of the dark forces that there is no Light, and sometimes when we work in this realm, we connect with the thought/feel of hopeless separateness. So, we want to anchor in our hearts and in the Divine, inside and out. We want to hold information about the dark forces not with fascination, but for transformation and initiation.[114]

If we can hold the bigger picture of the darkness, it's role and how it works, we can approach these realms with more clarity and less fear. At a deep level, evil is a defense against pain. It's temporary and present on this plane to teach—that is, darkness is ultimately in service to the Light.

As we learn to hold from our center the way darkness shows up in our psyche, emotions, actions and energy field, we can use the knowledge of the deep function of the contracted state as the key to unlock the Divine. That is, "I cannot know oneness if I haven't known separateness." "If I haven't been hurt, I cannot learn forgiveness."

Evil teaches us to cherish and choose love, if we learn from it. At the same time, it's an energy that's destructive for its own sake, materialistic, masterfully uses half-truth, insists on its self-will (always

---

114. See Glossary

"going for" separation), and it wants to stay hidden. It wants to stay hidden because, in general, when we're conscious of something "off" in ourselves, we tend to let it go immediately.

Darkness influences us through our faults and lower self. This is the place we all want to run from. We're afraid we won't be loved if we're negative. We're also afraid if we open our awareness to it, we'll "become" totally dark. Awakening to the true darkness that we carry is what we fear most in life, not anything from the outside. Our "pure" darkness (straight out "I want to kill you" not rationalized as "you're wrong.") is a defense against pain and a "no" to love and life. The revelation and harmonization of these energies is a vital step in finding the love we're all longing for. We can be earnest and even vehement in our conscious minds about following spirit, but if we don't find the hidden "no," we'll always have a "cap" or ceiling to our spiritual potential.

Not only is darkness in service to the Light, it's the inversion of the Light.

It is *the reversal that catalyzes the memory of the Truth.* Through the capacity to hold opposites—understanding paradox—we can use the catalyst of the dark to transform. For instance, poverty is the inversion of abundance. They are the same energy, one is in its healthy state, and one is a twist of the healthy energy. If you carry a poverty consciousness, you're learning about abundance. If you have the capacity for great poverty, you have the capacity for great abundance. It's a teaching that you came in to learn.

This is not to beat yourself up because you haven't gotten it right, but rather to hold yourself in compassion and begin to learn about the wound[115] that created the misconception about God's abundance.

Evil is allowed to exist because we have free will. We are, and have been, free to create and choose what we wish, light or dark. In order to choose wisely on this path to oneness, we must be grounded in the healthy ego, *then* a seeker or initiate. The incarnational chakras, the first three, support the spiritual chakras.

---

115. See Format for Healing

The characteristics of darkness are destruction, half-truth and materialism.[116]

The levels of darkness and the light are many. There's a hierarchy of both, and they both exist in other dimensions.[117] There are realms of much greater density than the earth plane and much less density. The earth is the plane of 50% darkness, 50% light. Many levels of beings,[118] both light and dark, affect us according to our receptivity (beliefs about the nature of life/God).

It's a spiritual law[119] that we must ask for help from the realms of light because they will not transgress, and because we have free will. There's a hierarchy of angelic beings available for our protection, enlightenment and healing. In addition to our guardian, our guides (which change as we progress), and a host of angels around us, we can call on the Archangels and the Masters. Christians feel especially connected to the Master Jesus; Buddhists are connected to Lord Buddha, etc.

If you pay attention, you'll notice that the angelic forces are helping you all the time. In my experience, when there is synchronicity and/or explicit timing, there's often angelic help afoot. A common sign that angels are near is a fragrant scent that has no overt source.

The Forces of Light as well as the forces of darkness talk to us. As you open, heal, and ask for help, you become aware that you're receiving assistance, even about mundane things. We often ignore this help with contradictions from our ego mind. I remember once receiving a message as I was going upstairs (a long flight) to see my grandchildren. A voice said, "Take your glasses." I said in return, "I won't need them." Well, of course, I did need them and had to make another trip down and up that big flight of stairs! I always apologize when I argue and don't listen, and I thank them for their help.

The dark energies will violate our field with their loudness, bullying and seduction. The entities and other dark forms are "called"

---

116. Pathwork Lecture #248, "Three Principles of the Forces of Evil—Personification of Evil"

117. See Additional Materials, Dimensions and Planes

118. Ibid

119. See Spritual Laws

vibrationally by the dense energy produced by our misconceptions, defenses, fears, faults and traumas. There are no victims, however. Like attracts like, and the density holds a teaching. Conversely, our requests, our harmonic beliefs, our work on ourselves, our prayers, and any positive energy that we have mentally, emotionally, physically and spiritually, "calls" the Forces of Light. The outer reflects the inner. Inside us we have both going on, as we well know.

We need help in finding our "receptor sites"[120] to the dense energies and releasing them from our field, that is, our energetic field, our emotional body, our mental body and other levels of our aura. There is an energetic form[121] in our body and/or field that carries a misconception, the emotional charge and defense against pain. The energetic form also has a color and vibratory level. For instance, the vibration of the belief that "God loves me but abuses me," will draw an entity that carries this negative mixture—a like vibration—and, we'll also draw people to us that carry this energy—this is the medicine for the healing. Another way that we may be "receptive" is when we "unleash" into some form of negativity. For instance, if we allow ourselves to act out our anger, or jealousy, or vindictiveness, we can channel a dark entity—that is, we let it come through us.

Any activity where we "leave" our bodies, like alcoholism or drug addiction, will also draw negative energies. Places where these activities occur will tend to "harbor" negative energies. By the same token, places where people sincerely pray and meditate will be a gathering place for the angels of light. Even in your imagination you can feel the difference in the energy, if you imagine walking into an opium den, and then onto a deserted beach at dawn...

In working with entities, it's necessary to have someone to help you heal the mental/emotional/energetic misconception and release the "hitch hiker." We need help, not only to see through any blind spots in our mental/emotional bodies, but because we cannot go home alone. Also, when we work with someone, our light together is synergistic. The light is many times more powerful than the dark, but most of us are not purified enough and can get caught in illu-

---

120. See Glossary, Format for Healing
121. See Approaching Healing Energetically

sion through our fears and misconceptions. Therefore, find someone
who is a little further on the path than you are. This is the Law of
Brotherhood,[122] and the manifestation of the Truth of the connectedness of all things.

I offer the following about releasing entities for your information. You can't do it alone. To release an entity, hold the highest point
of light you can, call for help from the Forces of Light (the Entity
Police, St. Michael, The Mighty Rescue Spirits of Light, et. al.), work
with the receptor site (mental/emotional/energetic contraction), and
release the entity(s) from the body and/or field and send them back
where they came from. Dark entities, demons, etc., come from another realm and they must be sent back where they belong so they
don't attach to someone else. It's necessary to heal the wound that
allowed the energy in, or we'll draw a similar energy.

We neither resist nor engage with dark energies. So we don't try
to "save" the dark entity from itself. If you're unsure as to whether or
not an energy is dark, ask if it's in the Christ Consciousness. It *must*
answer truthfully. Another time when you want to ask this question is
when you begin to be aware of getting messages from higher beings
(teachers). Sometimes a dark entity will masquerade as a being of
light. A tip-off here is when you get a feeling or thought that something may not be right, and/or they appeal to the "little ego."

There are different kinds of dark beings. Some are "elemental" in
nature, that is, beings that can be directed to fulfill a task—of course,
in the realm of pain and suffering. (I have seen these levels as insec-
toid or animal-like). Then there are dark beings that are more intelligent. They may be experts[123] of lust, addiction, jealousy, etc. They're
drawn to like vibrations. Therefore, where we have faults, we'll draw
an entity of similar vibration. They will "feed" off emotions and exaggerate them, "talk" to us and try to exploit our weakness and keep us
enmeshed. You'll notice here that they are limited to *influencing* us
through our own negative places. They can't overpower against our
light.

The lower energies are nothing new in our experience, we've

122. See Spiritual Laws
123. See Glossary

"heard" these voices in our heads, we just thought it was us. Again, there are no victims—we draw energies with like vibrations. It's helpful to know what may be happening in other dimensions that may be influencing us.

While we want to aspire to being the undefended heart, until we have adequate protection with our love, it's necessary to pay attention to clearing our body, our field and our space regularly.[124]

So, it doesn't serve us to go into the separation with the forces of darkness. We can stand in our sincerity and light and know that it's our teacher. It's a part of us and a part of God on this plane of earth duality. It's a temporary energy. It's neither for us to resist or engage—resistance is contraction in itself and what you resist gets stronger; engaging can so easily become fighting and forcing. We must learn its lessons in order to move higher, and "just say no."

And again, the light is infinitely more powerful than the dark. While it takes a while to learn about the complexities of the realm of darkness, that's only because we've closed our awareness to it. It's important and prudent to know the territory.

The ray of light that we connect with in our minds and hearts scatters to the four winds the most enmeshed mess of dark energies.

Remember, the lotus grows from the mud.

"So magnificently sovereign is our Lover; never say,
"On the other side of this river a different king rules,"
For how could that be true—for nothing can oppose Infinite
*   strength.*

No one lives outside the walls of this sacred place, existence.

The holy water my soul's brow needs is unity.
Love opened my eye and I was cleansed
by the purity of each
form.

St. Francis of Assisi

---

124. See Additional Materials, Energetic Clearing and Protection

KINDNESS/RATIONALIZATION

None of us think of ourselves as unkind people. What we do and say to others that they "have trouble with" is aimed, in our own minds, at "helping them." Sometimes we rationalize that we need to "overcome" their blindness by pushing "our truth" on them. Sometimes we need to "override" what they're saying with our own interpretation. Sometimes we have to "set someone straight" because they're so misguided. If we don't do it, then who will? Sometimes when there's a holiday or a birthday, we'll give the gift of a book about a subject that's important to us—perhaps something to do with our religion or way of life. All the while, in our own minds, thinking we're being good and kind. These behaviors come from an attitude of forcing "my way" on someone else. We rationalize our behavior out of a picture in our minds of who we think we are. We're good and kind, and we just know better.

At times, we set ourselves up to be judge, jury and executioner. We harden our heart toward a daughter, son, husband, or friend because of their life choices or their beliefs. We hold ourselves as good and righteous while we punish people by judging, withdrawing or pushing.

We get caught in the rationale of the mind and don't realize we're acting out negative impulses. When we strip away all the "reasons" (ours!) we find that we're in fact "spending" our energy for something we didn't sign up for in our conscious mind.

When we ask ourselves with sincerity and with a willingness to strip away the rationale, the "*because*", "what am I doing with my energy?" we'll find the fundamental truth of what we *are* in fact doing. We're so used to couching our thoughts, words, emotions and actions in all our reasons, that we fail to notice what is right up front—sometimes we're being cruel, in thought, word or deed. What we're doing is really all that matters, not our reasons. That is what we will have to answer for in the end. When we pass into the next dimension and drop the physical body, we'll look back on our lives and see clearly what we did, thought, and felt. Those energies have form and they affect people—and us, who sent it. The question won't be about who was right about what or our feelings about it, or "why" we did what we did, it will be about who we are, what energies we sent out into the universe, where we loved and where we didn't love.

The place we want to look for in ourselves is where we can let go of being right and open to the spaciousness of allowing. Others are on a journey to oneness also, and they're doing the best they can. We're not all in the same place at the same time in our evolution toward harmony, but we're definitely all drawn to find peace and love. We want to practice being conscious to the other, and ourselves we want to "make" goodness, kindness, comfort, peace, and love. When we're not "making" we're "undoing" or destroying.

Ask yourself the question, "what am I doing with my energy," before you pass over. Make it a way of life.

"Kindness in words creates confidence.
Kindness in thinking creates profoundness.
Kindness in giving creates love."

Lao Tzu

"My religion is very simple. My religion is kindness."

The Dalai Lama

HUMILITY/SPLENDIDNESS

Well, these two certainly seem like opposites, don't they? And, yet again, we come to paradox. We need both.

Humility has a mass consciousness meaning of meekness, poor, lowliness unimportant, weak. When we speak of spiritual humility, however, we don't mean weak or unimportant, we mean a state that recognizes that we are not above, but are like everyone else in fundamental ways. That is, we're all evolving toward a common place, oneness; we all have a human body, we're all fallible, we all inhabit this dualistic plane where we struggle to grow. Spiritual humility, which the Bible calls "meekness," means that we don't succumb to hatred or negativity. This meekness doesn't mean that we let the negativity of others play out on us. We can draw a boundary. But, it does mean that we're centered in a state of being that is not attached to acting out our negativity, and deeper, that we're not harboring thoughts and emotional reactions that are negative.

Spiritual humility also carries the expanded consciousness of recognizing that we are not linear beings. While we may have mastered to a great degree, or are at least in deep witness to, our negative thoughts, words, and actions and embody a state of compassion; we can also find ourselves in states of complete regression into insecurity, hatred, and malice. We fluctuate back and forth. We are a dynamic being that exists on many levels of consciousness at once. We are generally "based" in one, that is, we live most of our life there.

Looking at the states of consciousness of the chakras[125] is a good way to understand the levels of consciousness of mankind. So, if we hold a state of being that rests, for instance, in the heart chakra, we can navigate the wounded child[126] more quickly and efficiently, than if your consciousness is based in the third chakra. If you're primarily based in your third, you may spend a lot of time in the pain and defense level and have a more difficult time coming out.

If your state of being is in the heart chakra, you'll have higher spiritual experiences, hold more equanimity, peace and love—and be working on the fears and woundings of the higher chakras. We'll keep piercing through to higher and higher levels of consciousness until our basic state of being raises to the next level, in this case, the throat chakra.

With the recognition, from our center and not our wounded ego, that we're at once masters and crying children, it's impossible to judge someone else. The heart holds everything with compassion and can recognize as illusion any parts that are not there.

Most difficult, amazingly, is our ability to see and accept our splendidness. Our wounded ego makes us special in myriad ways; but the clear, present, grounded realization of our beauty and light is a place that we embody only piece by piece. We're blinded by our specialness that the unhealed ego holds onto for dear life. It actually takes a great deal of courage to put aside the clinging to our "little

---

125. See Additional Materials, Chakra Consciousness
126. See Format for Healing

ego" that wants to be separate and better, and embrace the glory of our splendidness; our lighted, loving, essential nature. While we may have difficulty making a list of our faults, it's even more difficult to make a list of our virtues. Many of us, if we ever have to write a bio for publicity purposes or even a resume, need someone else to write about our good qualities and strengths. (Or perhaps we hold the other pole of always affirming to ourselves and others how "great" we are, all the while denying the unworthiness underneath).

We need to take the blinders off, to be in reality about who we really are. We need to "stand in" our love, our beauty, our kindness, our generosity, our wisdom, and our power. We need to *identify* ourselves as this—truly know this is who we are. Now, from this foundation— this true foundation—we can embody more deeply our Loving Witness. When this happens, we are in the "fast lane" of spiritual growth. And, we can see from this vantage point—the top of the hill instead of in a rabbit hole in the valley of our wounding—a greater Reality. When we inhabit the Loving Witness, we can do our inner work from a compassionate wisdom grounded in the Reality of the deep love of the heart. As we uncover profound layers of love in our hearts, the splendid being that we are shines through all the layers, and finally the personality.

This process is one we haven't been prepared for. Here we are connecting with this incredible being that we are, and at the same time realizing that parts of us can still land in the pit of our anger and fear! We can feel our vibration shifting into this amazing resonance one moment, and the next moment we are charged with a judgment. Keeps you honest.

By embodying this splendid, lighted, loving energy that heals people by your very presence *and* the wounded, wretched being sending out negative energy with your thoughts and/or emotions, we begin to walk the world as a master. A master is not someone who is clear of doubts or negativity, but rather accepts deeply the imperfections as well as the beauty. The master is a spiritual warrior that walks forward to meet fear, adversity, and "danger." The master doesn't hurt anybody.

And, again, we're not talking about a state of being that gets turned on like a light switch. Mastery[127] is a *process* with a full spectrum from none to complete. We move along slowly—most of us—clearing, opening, building our light-body, purifying. Somewhere, as we're moving along in this process, we come to a place in the spectrum where an abiding peace and joy comes in. And then, we walk around with it a lot. Sometimes it's interrupted with another lesson, but it can be recaptured. The secret to recapturing it becomes clearer and stronger, we give up and let go, again and again, of our habitual negative patterns and look for the love. We say to ourselves, "I'm not going to stay in the pain of this illusion. Whatever cherished beliefs and habits I have to let go of, I'll do it. I want to take that armor off my heart and be in the truth of the love." We consciously turn toward living with self-honesty, integrity and compassion with the world and ourselves. We're willing to go inside and ask our hearts what the Truth is, and then we're willing to die for it –mentally, emotionally or physically. We do what we have to do and we take what comes. We never support lies, deceit or negativity, either by action or non-action. We are kind. We can witness ourselves. We know ourselves to be a part of everyone and everything, and we long to serve. This is our splendidness.

So, as we do our inner work, we carry our humility and our splendidness together. We love more.

Our capacity to love in this moment—now, is the truest picture of where we are on the path.

> *"Our deepest fear is not that we are inadequate.*
> *Our deepest fear is that we are powerful beyond measure.*
>
> *It is our light, not our darkness, that most frightens us.*
> *We ask ourselves, "Who am I to be Brilliant, Gorgeous, Talented*
> *   and Fabulous?"*
>
> *Who are you **not** to be?*
>
> *You are a child of the Universe.*

---

127. See Glossary

Your playing small does not serve the world.

There is nothing enlightened about shrinking
so that other people won't feel insecure around you.

We were born to make manifest
the Glory of the Universe that is within us.

It's not just in some of us, It is in **everyone**.

As we let our own light shine,
we unconsciously give other people permission to do the same.

As we are liberated from our own fear,
our presence automatically liberates others."[128]

---

128. *Nelson Mandella (1994 Inaugural Speech)*

Format for Healing:

This process will help you to "connect the dots" in your healing process:

Life manifestation—disharmony
to wounded child—the human emotional level
to soul's teaching—the issue with life/God

This is not so much a set of "steps" as points of awareness in the process of healing. They can be done in any order.

Each point needs to be given its full time. It may not be appropriate to touch all the points at one time when an issue is up. This is fine. It's the depth and thoroughness of the process that's important. And, at each point of awareness, connect to the *feeling* level, or you will be in the disconnected mind.

It's always good to do this exploration with help, but if you're alone, it may be helpful to write your experience at each interval of energy coming into balance—when you reach a plateau. Although you can use any order in the format, connecting with your inner center should always be first—not only first for a healing, but the primary focus of your day.

As you center[129] within yourself, the container from which we heal is the manager on the adult ego level, and the Godself from the spiritual level—the Loving Witness that evolves into greater and greater light.

1. Turning to the inner guide[130]

This is a place that you know, although you may not have called it your Inner guide. You may have called it your intuition or your conscience.

The difference here, is that we're not waiting for the "knowing" to

---

129. See Processes, Finding Your Center
130. See Glossary

come in but are using our positive will to connect with it and also to make it a consistent and strong part of our lives.

There are many terms for this level of consciousness and many levels of this term: adult, manager, guide, witness, Higher Self, Godwoman, and Godman. I like Godwoman/man because it embodies the maturity of the adult, the objectivity of the Witness and connection to the highest vibration of love and compassion you can reach. I *find this energy in my deep heart* (the outer layers of the heart have wounding, but if you venture deep into the heart chakra you'll find a place that's beyond human wounding and attachments). For me, it looks like a ball of white light with the consciousness of God's love. This is the place from which you ask, "What is the Truth?" This level of Truth is, of course, Truth with a capital "T"—*the Truth beyond self-interest, that is compassionate, clear and loving.* The clarity of this level sees darkness, but knows that it's our teacher, knows we all have it, is not in fear or judgment of it, and has compassion for those caught temporarily in it's web—including ourselves!

Sometimes it may feel more powerful to use different aspects of (or layers) of this energy in different situations. For instance, if you're caught in big emotions from your wounded child, it may be most palpable in that moment to look for the adult. The concept of God may be too remote for the raging infant. It may need the mother up front, with God coming through her. You can use the signal of anger, fear, and upset –the unpleasant emotions—to let yourself know that you're in the child consciousness. You might say to yourself, "Ok, I feel this strongly, and yet I know it comes from my history, it's an over-reaction—where is my adult?" "What would the good mother/father say?" "What does the child need?"

With practice, you'll find your Godman easily. And, with time you'll get accustomed to the feeling of "rightness" it has, and to the fact that this is the Real you.

We *connect with our inner guide through practice*; that is, *meditation* and *conscious activation.* When you're meditating, call forth your Godwoman/man; sit with it. When it feels palpable—and this may take a number of sittings—ask a question and allow the answer to come in. Try not to be attached to the answer or how it shows itself.

You may experience it as a thought, kinesthetically, emotionally or through sensing.[131]

2. Find a disharmony

The disharmony might be *a feeling, thoughts, physical problems, a situation, or a person.*

3. Connecting to history

(a) We connect to our history by searching our memories for the *same feeling as a child* that we are experiencing now in the disharmonious situation. We find, as we make this connection, that there is a *pattern* in our lives of similar situations and/or feelings about people.

(Our wounded child recreates the pain of childhood; always trying to get what it needed back then. This is a futile endeavor, however, because this space in the child can never be filled from the outside. If someone comes close to satisfying the need of the wounding, it will never be good enough. We have to do our healing from the inside out).

Whenever we have an emotional reaction to a situation, we're in the past in the child consciousness. We must unfreeze those places that are stuck in the past and reproduce it over and over. We access the child consciousness through the emotions and disharmonious situations it produces, and it's necessary to listen deeply and intently to take in what is going on.

Sometimes a photograph of you as a small child can be a window, psychologically and energetically, to accessing the climate of your home of origin and the emotions that have been locked up.

(b) Once we've discovered the emotional link, we can go deeper

---

131. When we get to a certain stage of healing, we become aware of the outer guide coming through with guidance. This is a highly developed spirit that makes itself known to help and teach us. There is also "direct knowing" that comes through the crown into the brain. With outer guides, it's important to surrender to the teaching, but also to retain your autonomy—the truth in the paradox again.

by asking ourselves *questions*: What were the circumstances? Was it father or mother? Remember the details.

(c) *Let the emotions come.* The feelings must be *felt fully*. Explore from your feeling center (as best you can, without judgment) layer upon layer.

The child may want to punish him/her—make them totally at fault and pound them to a bloody pulp until they admit they are bad and wrong!

This is a layer. Try to stay with the raw feelings as much as possible and let go of the story. (Although, if you haven't told your story to anyone, it is important to be heard) Often anger[132] will come first, or bitterness, fear or hatred.

Sometimes the reaction of the child is to collapse into the hurt. This child is the victim and believes he has no power—which it did not in the past. Sometimes the child will tend to submit to the "aggressor." In each case, it's necessary for healing to help the child "stand up" and allow the strong emotions up.

Let them all come up and move out in a safe way.[133]

When you're emptied out,[134] *the pain can come to the surface.* Now you've hit gold. This is what was driving the blame, maligning, judgment, and punishment. You didn't want to feel the hurt. *The hurt from the present situation is the same hurt from childhood.* Allow as much time as is needed.

When you reach a plateau, see if you can *translate the emotions into words*. Try to make a simple statement.

4. Naming the belief

As you get through the emotions of the childhood situation, intend to bring in your Loving Witness. (Allow yourself to be open to awareness of the feelings of the child and the energy of the witness at the same time). The witness (Godwoman/man) can bring in an objective, loving presence to get clear about *the precise belief (misconceptions)*

132. See Processes, Working with Anger
133. See Processes, Working with Emotions
134. Ibid

that arose in the child as a result of it's wounding. It may be, "I'm bad & wrong, not good enough, flawed, not acceptable, unlovable, a failure." These wrong beliefs create our lives. They are beliefs about the world, not just about Mom, but also about all women. These wrong beliefs create the disharmonies of our lives.

5. Leaving "the other" behind consciously

This is the place where we *release the other from the grip of our defensive posture.*

As you look again at the disharmony in the present, you'll want to *summarize* what happened and get beneath the "story" of what has been "done to you." Keep sifting through what "he said" and what "she said" until you can isolate the "bare bones" facts, without your feelings about it or your reasons. For instance, "he said something that hurt me." The next step is to realize that *you are responsible for what you are feeling.* You create your own hurt. If you didn't have a wound about such and such, you would notice that the person said something thoughtless or even cruel, but it would not hurt you. This awareness changes our reality significantly. (Although the child consciousness has many details of what happened that will all "prove" the other is "guilty." This is blame. Blame is a blind alley. It takes you into a negative cycle.

What's needed is to let go of the outside that we've been conditioned to focus on, and *turn inward* to *find your part.* It may even be as little as 1%, but it *always takes two* to create a disharmony. Ask yourself the question: "What did I do, think, say, etc., that brought this in?" (This is from the energetic, spiritual level, not the unhealed ego that may have a tendency to take "all the blame" on yourself).

Now, we're coming into the Reality of the present situation.

In the last analysis, the other is only our "sacred trigger." Our real work is inside when we have an emotional reaction to something. If we focus on the other, we're following a negative voice that wants to keep us stuck. It's when we've done our inner healing, that we go to the other to confront negative behavior. If we're not in our intention to get closer to them, we're not ready to confront. When we're ready to go to the person, we reveal ourselves—not expecting them to take care of our wounded child—and make our boundaries, if necessary. For example, "When you said such and such, I got hurt." You're not making the other person bad and wrong, and you own your emotions.

As we embody this process honestly, we discover that the other person is innocent—even if they have done something negative. That is, they don't deserve our punishment.

6. The real meaning of the problem

Once we've let go of our enmeshment with "the other," owning our emotions and are seeing the disharmony more clearly, we can open to the fact that the real meaning of this, and any, "problem" is that *it is a catalyst for your deep healing.* That does not mean that the other hasn't transgressed, or that you don't need to draw a boundary, or that you're not hurt by his/her actions. It does mean, however, that you're viewing life differently: you're not a victim; you know your emotions are yours; you're willing to let go of the negativity that uses someone's transgression as sanction to defend; you've come to a place in your evolvement where you consciously choose to learn and heal; you see things more clearly; and your understanding opens the door to compassion.

7. Healing the Habitual Pattern—The Signal

After you've stepped through your healing, look back to the point of being catalyzed by the person or situation to find a feeling, thought or body sensation that comes up just as you're entering the emotional reaction. This is *your inner signal of the outer catalyst.* For instance, if someone insinuates that you're not enough, you may get a clenching in your stomach. The clenching sensation is your signal that you're being triggered—that is, catapulted into the emotions of the past. Another signal might be "fire in the belly"—immediate anger; or a sense of immobility, like a deer in the headlights. There will be times when you miss the early signal and find yourself in your defense. Have mercy for yourself, and stop as soon as you can—make amends, then go inside and do your inner healing work.

When you're aware that your signal is activated, consciously intend to connect *with your Godwoman/man and witness yourself in the
old, illusory paradigm.* What I say to myself is, "This is illusion. I'm not
seeing this situation clearly."This helps me to get a little objective distance and stops the habitual pattern of reaction. It may often happen
that you have the mental distance, but your emotions are still bouncing
off the walls. This happens sometimes. Wait it out. Pray. Be in your intention to say "no" to the compulsion to go into the emotional pull of
the illusion again, and do your best to tolerate holding both energies
at the same time. The emotions will dissipate, usually within a few
minutes. The thing to be aware of here is that it's ok and part of your
process of healing to have uncomfortable emotions. There's nothing
wrong. It's important to *make your peace with the fact that discomfort
is one of the things we have in this life sometimes.* There's a wonderful
quote that helps me, "Pain is inevitable. Suffering is optional."[135]

This process is one of breaking a much-used and strong habitual
pattern to "react" into your defense. Once you bring your energy to it
one time, and stop the momentum of the habit, it will get easier.

This is doing aikido[136]—using the energy of the emotional reaction as a signal to turn the disharmony into healing.

8. Healing the Child

Paramount to healing the child is finding the *real need* that didn't
get satisfied in childhood. If the wound is that you're not enough, the
Godwoman/man brings in the Truth to that immature and frozen
part of you.

The false need may be to punish, to complain, to withdraw, to submit or to aggress. The real need may be to accept yourself, to know that
there is enough for you, to know that you're loved and connected.

Here is where the core of the matter is addressed. The Godwoman
holds the space of the loving parent/angel that the child needed in
the past. It gives emotionally the support, acceptance, nurturance, and

---

135. Kathleen Casey Theisen, *Each Day a New Beginning, Daily Meditations for
Women* (Center City, MN: Hazelden Educational Materials, 1982) November
14.

136. See Glossary

connection that the child was longing for and didn't get from the parent. This healing doesn't just come from the mind, but is transmitted from the heart to him. It's a strongly held *feeling* level of the Truth—"you are totally accepted and cherished exactly the way you are, because of the way you are." This is the embodiment of the *feeling Truth that is brought to the feeling of the untruth.*

The inner child, frozen in a painful place, feels the experience of being protected, helped and loved in addition to learning the harmonious Reality of the specific issue. Energetically, this is the healing process of bringing light where there is no light.

Now, you're not abandoning your inner child by having it handle the uncomfortable situation, again. You're *using your positive will to connect with the highest consciousness you are capable of, and bringing the child into the energy of the love of that higher consciousness.*

9. Finding Alignment

After we have come through the healing process, we pay attention again to centering, which creates alignment. Alignment is a context for holding this process of healing. That is, understanding and intending to bring in the highest level of the order of consciousness (chakric consciousness) that we can attain at the moment. Ultimately, the highest order of consciousness occurs when *all our energies are in service to the heart.* In this healing process we want to bring in consciousness that says, "I intend to focus for a moment on *aligning my chakras* (levels of consciousness). I am my God/woman/man in my heart holding my child in my second chakra. *I can be aware and feel two levels of consciousness at the same time.* I can hold all of who I am. I am a multi-faceted being that carries diverse levels of consciousness: Love, compassion, beauty, peace, negativity, and an intent to hurt. I am all these things and at any given moment, I choose which way to go. I either take the hand of my higher consciousness or my lower consciousness."

10. Connecting with the Soul Level

Our soul's misconception about God/life is transferred[137] onto our parents. We experience the mental/emotional levels of that misconception through our child. In the healing process we track the wrong belief and emotional charge catalyzed by the disharmonic situation back to the soul level for the teaching about life/God. For example, say the misconception at the soul level is that we're not worthy of God—not good enough for God's favor. At the soul level, we "forgot" that Real love is unconditional. Therefore, we choose parents that will stimulate that wound so that in this incarnation, we can experience the pain of it and heal.

This part is not just a mental exercise. The mind is used to bring our awareness to the emotions of the wound with our parents, and from that mental/emotional place, we look at how it expands into a belief about all of life (God). As our inner guide (Godwoman/man) brings the healing to the emotional wounding of the child, the child not only heals a specific wound, but experiences by osmosis that there *is* help—there *is* a God, and by implication, *I am a part of it*. The soul remembers the harmony of the Truth.

Then, working directly with spirit, we ask to be *infused with the feeling* and realization of unconditional love. *We "remember" the Truth of the reality of things.* By "remembering" I mean the healing of the place where we "forgot" an aspect of the fundamental makeup of the universe/life/God. We let go of the tightness of fear and pseudo-protection against being hurt, and we let go of the mistaken idea that somehow we are outside of everything and that we are judged. We breathe into our emotional, mental and spiritual bodies the Reality of love. We "remember" the deep connection with each other, that love is truly unconditional, that we are all one, and reclaim our rightful place within the unity of God. We "remember" that we're a part of God, that without us the universe would crumble. We are needed and we have a purpose. This is not an ego place, but a humble (and blissful) state of being that knows its value and purpose.

Therefore, as we traverse the peaks and valleys of our healing, a major touchstone is *finding the Divine that has become inverted*. Medi-

---

137. See Additional Materials, Transference/Counter-Transference

tating with this—asking our guides to help us *"feel" the healed energy in our mental, emotional, physical and spiritual bodies.* Work with this often. If you have trouble feeling the energy, ask your guides to "turn up the volume" for you.

A cornerstone of our deep healing is turning to the spiritual, *what is it my soul is trying to remember?*

Approaching Healing Energetically

We can approach the process of healing at the spiritual level, psycho-emotional level or at the energetic level, or a blend of all three. It's helpful and expansive to connect with the issue energetically because it can give you a little distance on the emotional charge of the problem, an awareness of who you really are (light), and experience with those worlds we cannot see with our physical eyes.

Every thought, emotion, word and action are manifested as a form with a certain frequency, sound, color and odor. Therefore, the clairvoyant can "see" the form of what you're thinking and feeling, as well as the form of a disharmonic pattern or disease. Of course, your love, centeredness, kindness and all your good qualities can also be seen—as well as felt in the body.

In learning to "read" energy, our imagination is our bridge. We've been taught to ignore our imagination or to have disdain for it. The right use of the imagination, that is without forcing or negative intent but as an instrument for opening our perceptions, can help us to "view" the unseen worlds.

To begin, center yourself and create a sacred circle.[138]

It's helpful in understanding and getting inside an energy to feel the emotion of the "problem" and find where that emotion lives in the body. From here, you can imagine what that energy may look like—color, size, texture. Clear colors indicate a healthy energy, muddied or black indicates a contracted energy. The form of the energy holds the emotional charge, misconception, wound and healing of the issue.

Now you can still feel the emotions, but you have a little distance and can get some information that will help you get to the root of the issue. With your awareness and intention, you can penetrate the energy, like a hot knife through butter. (You can also imagine a part of yourself very small so you can walk into the energy) You are the sovereign of your body and field, and energies "want" to open. Ask for

---

138. See Glossary

its *statement of consciousness*, i.e., the statement could be, "I must close my heart to the man or he will hurt me".

As you tune into energies, you will become aware of the level of vibration they carry. Discordant energies may feel uncomfortable in your body or to your senses. They may feel jagged or prickly, or you may feel the need to gag. Energetically, they have a coarse, slowed-down vibration, muddy colors, and smell bad. They are contracted energy that is held—immobile. On the psychological level, they are misconceptions about life. They are negative, heavy, slow, limited and have little understanding. On the emotional level, they are painful and compulsive. On the spiritual level, they are misconceptions about the nature of God.

As you focus your attention (its also very effective to touch the energy with your hand) you may feel an emotion or "see" a picture on your mind-screen. Follow whatever information comes up, noting each piece and using it to point to the next. For instance, if you feel a prickly sensation on your skin, you might ask, "what is this energy saying?" If it's saying, "I'm afraid," you might ask "what are you afraid of?" It might say, "Someone is going to humiliate me." You would ask, "Who?" And continue to follow the opening and decoding of the energy. There will be a temptation to go to your mind to "figure out" what the answer might be. If/when this happens, keep bringing yourself back to the focus of the energy. You want to let the energy "speak" and not interpret from your particular perceptual reality. This information is in your unconscious, and that may not fit your conscious mind-set.

You know the trajectory of your healing,[139] so keep it in mind. The human source of the wound is in your childhood, and the spiritual source is the misconception of the soul.

As you work through the wrong beliefs and the emotions connected to them from your history, you'll begin to feel/see/know the Truth. You can ask your guides and any expert healers in the Christ Consciousness to bring in healing for this issue. You may "see" the colors clear up. And, you'll get a sense of a shift into a harmonic vibration. You can use your intention to connect your energy with

---

139. See Format for Healing

the higher vibratory levels of peace, gratitude, and love (and all the essential energies of God, the Virtues). [140]

This process of learning what is inside us and bringing healing to it is like Jedi Training. It's rigorous, rewarding and it leads us to something greater than what we thought to be ourselves. We're training ourselves out of density into the holding of the higher vibrational states of bliss and the oneness of God. We're training ourselves out of duality and into harmony.

As we become more aware of how energy looks, feels and acts, the range of our experience widens and we, therefore, have more responsibility. Since energy follows thought, we become aware of how powerful a thought is. Our thoughts have form and they go to the people we're thinking about, be it positive or negative. If the thought is in the harmony of the loving universe, the accompanying energy, for yourself and others—emotional experience, physical experience— is harmonious, feels good. If the thought is out of harmony, then the accompanying energy is constricted and painful. This is the way energy works. This is the science of God. Anything out of harmony is uncomfortable. The same is true of our emotions. Hence, we need deep training to reorient ourselves in relationship to our thoughts and emotions. We need to recognize that we're responsible not only for what we say and do, but what we think and feel.

As this process of change unfolds, the energetic contractions (densities) in our field[141] gradually get transmuted—that is, the dense energy is untwisted and returns to its natural state, a harmonic energy. The color changes from a muddied one—or black—into pure hues. The vibration changes from a coarse/dense vibration to a lighter frequency. Therefore, our field becomes lighter and lighter, more and more beautiful, and a positive cycle of healing gets created that builds our light body. As our vibratory level gets higher and higher, the lower density vibrations cannot live in the same space and certain energies simply leave our field. Therefore, when situations/persons ignite the wounding behind the dark colors and dense frequencies of fear and hatred, we find that we cannot so easily go into the fight anymore.

---

140. See Glossary
141. Ibid

The shoe is too tight. We're better able to turn to the higher way. We have a greater capacity to hold both the "old way" (reactions of the lower emotions) and the new way—the positive *and* negative, and then to align with the positive. The thrall of duality has been broken. We move into a deeper integration within as we consciously turn to love. This isn't done from a denial of what in us needs to be purified, but rather from a deep commitment to return to harmony.

We're lighter, in mind, body, emotions and soul. We've entered the state of being where we're concerned with the inner, with love, with service.

This approach dovetails well with "The Pattern for Healing"

Conclusion

There are various touchstones to be aware of as we walk the path of deep purification and embodiment of our light.

First, this is a *path of consciousness*. God is consciousness supreme. Evolution is evolution in consciousness. We are a unique conscious spirit that never dies.

We find that when we stand in our love and look at the best and worst in us, we are *learning the territory* of a healing path through earth life. Our sense of things may shift and change as we evolve, but from the experience of turning inward, we know that we're going in the right direction. We discover who we are and why we're here.

Deep purification work is a *training*. During this training, our Higher Self/Witness/Real Self gets uncovered, moves into prominence as the Center of our identity. This Center holds the space for the unhealed ego to die. The part of the soul that's in pain and misconception about the nature of the universe has gotten drawn into a whirlwind of energy made up of the wounded child consciousness and all the disparate parts that are cast adrift and cannot connect up. We have to train ourselves out of this negativity and illusion. This is an act of positive will and it's hard work.

In this evolvement, we soon learn that we must *let go of the outside*, that is, attachments to things, people, our limited sense of "self." It's not necessary to forsake all connection to the world, however. It's there as our field of play, our stage, our teacher, and also as an amazing gift for love and pleasure. We must be awake to pick up its messages.

Our *perceptions* change. We consciously and joyously keep bringing our focus back to what is unitive and turn away from what is separative. Through this *practice*, our perception of ourselves and our world changes dramatically. We move from thinking of ourselves as alone, in pain and flawed, to identifying with our deep, compassionate mind/heart, our beauty and our love. We become the loving witness to our pain and negativities, and to our vast beauty and light. We go effortlessly now to our core for wisdom and truth, and to connect to the higher realms. This Real Self brings Wisdom, Love, Integration and Healing to the split-off child consciousness, the mask self, the lower self, the sub-personalities. From the comfort, strength and perception of the *Loving Witness*, we heal by *bridging* the various parts of ourselves into a congruent whole. This Witness deepens over time until we spend most of our time inhabiting the state of loving presence with others and ourselves. Our alive reality is no longer separateness and pain, but bliss. We hold ourselves and all life as precious.

Another shift in perception is our relationship to the past and future. We no longer rehash over and over what's already happened or fear what's coming. We bring our focus to *full presence in the moment*. We discover that this is the only moment, eternity. This is the place where everything is happening. It's what is alive and safe. It's where *you* are. It's where *God* is. Nothing else exists. This blessed, full and joyful Reality has always been there, right in front of us. We're training ourselves to perceive it and adapt our inner attitudes to the Harmony of it.

We move into a deep understanding of *free will*. We learn that we can *choose* light or dark, not with lip service or "for show" but *with our energy* from the heart. *Every choice is this choice.*

We discover that the real food is *spiritual food*. If we have that, we feel fulfilled. The real food comes from: high spiritual material of all kinds, human teachers, spiritual guides, others on the path, connection to our own Higher Self; and meditation. These help us stay connected to real meaning and stay on course.

We learn to *name things by their "right name,"* not our rationalization. This practice breaks open our shell of defense and brings us into clarity and Truth. In order to do this, we must be willing to look under what seems to be on the surface.

And, never to be forgotten, while we're fighting the battle with our darkness and uncloaking our light, the Divine comes in with *Grace*. We wake up one morning and the anger is gone—Or, you may be driving somewhere and a tide of joy touches your heart as realization comes in that you are happy and loved—Or, you have an experience of "knowing" your son forgives you for a mistake you made when he was young.

We are now in Reality; the Enlightenment of the realization that we are going back Home. We are evolving into *Harmony*, and finding that it was there all the time.

I pray that you question your reality with a light heart, and that you remember the oneness that is the Truth of your being.

Much Love,
Ann

Spiritual Laws[142]

"Divine Law is always just and fair. It is determined first and foremost by not hurting others.

Law in its real and divine sense has nothing to do with force and compulsion. Quite the contrary. As soon as force or compulsion sets in—whether it comes from outside or from within your own self—at that moment, divine law is violated. For divine law is inner freedom.

The learning and comprehension of these laws can take place only if one applies them first to the affected area of the personality."[143]

Law of Self-Responsibility
"You create your own reality."[144]

"Your life experiences are a reflection of the beliefs in your soul.

You should never believe for one instance that what you experience is unjust and unfair, no matter how much it may appear that way. In the last analysis, in absolute truth and reality, it is your misconception that has caused it."[145]

Law of Paying the Price
"There is a price to be paid for everything. He who tries to avoid this will finally pay much dearer."[146]

---

142. An additional source for Spiritual Laws is the Alice Bailey work. She talks about the "laws" in several of her books. One source is: Bailey, Alice A., *Esoteric Healing, A Treatise on the Seven Rays*, 10th printing (New York: Lucis Publishing Company, 1980)

143. From the "Anthology" of the Pathwork material

144. Pathwork Lecture #40, "More on Image Finding, Summary"

145. Pathwork Lecture #48, "The Life Force"

146. Pathwork Lecture #29, "Forces of Activity & Passivity—Finding God's Will"

"The disadvantageous side of each alternative or decision has to be faced and accepted."[147]

Law of Cause and Effect

Every act has its consequence in the sphere of present reality.

It is more difficult to see the same relationship between *thoughts and subtle attitudes*. The more developed person can perceive cause and effect on these less obvious levels."[148]

Law of Living in Truth

"To face life's reality means to face yourself as you are, with all your imperfections; embrace life whole-heartedly, without fear, without self-pity or being afraid of being hurt.

Say to yourself, "In order to become what I would like to be, I must first, without fear or shame or vanity, face what is in me."[149]

Law of Brotherhood

"To be able to open your heart to another brings spiritual help that you could not receive by yourself."[150]

"No matter how hard one works, how intelligently he reads or studies, no matter how much self-honesty one tries to have, if you are alone, you become locked up in a certain vacuum that bars a complete understanding and evaluation which flows automatically if aired to another soul. By remaining alone you violate the Law of Brotherhood in some subtle way. You also need a certain amount of humility to be able to talk openly about your difficulties, your weaknesses, your problems, as well as to receive criticism."[151]

---

147. Pathwork Lecture #32, "Decision Making"
148. Pathwork Lecture #245, "Cause & Effect on Various Levels of Consciousness"
149. Pathwork Lecture #25, "The Path, Initial Steps, Preparation & Decisions"
150. Pathwork Lecture #2, "Decisions and Tests"
151. Pathwork Lecture #26, "Finding One's Faults"

"As long as you keep things hidden within you, it puts everything out of proportion (you exaggerate or underestimate).

The moment you open up to another person, this indicates an act of humility, at least towards that one person. You do not want to appear more perfect than you are at that moment with that person. Thus you show yourself as you are. And you feel better all of a sudden when you are able to see things differently."[152]

Law of Justice

"The imperfection which each human being has created for himself must now be the remedy, so to speak, through which he can regain the last perfection…God's justice makes use of human injustice in order to bring about ultimate justice."[153]

"…for whatsoever a man soweth, that shall he also reap."[154]

Law of Transformation of Negativity

"The strength with which your divinity can penetrate the ego structure and manifest depends on the degree evil has been transformed throughout the evolutionary development."[155]

Law of Lack of Awareness of One Area of Your Human Personality Prohibits Awareness of Another

"It is one of the immutable spiritual laws that lack of awareness of one area in you prohibits awareness of another. This is why the path purification process is conscious. This awareness unifies you. It is the

---

152. Pathwork Lecture #31, " Shame"

153. Pathwork Lecture #5, "Happiness for Yourself vs. Happiness as a Link in the Chain of Life"

154. Galatians 6:7 (KJV)

155. Pathwork Lecture #222, "Transformation of the Lower Self/Summary of the Year's Work"

aim of this Path's approach to spiritual reunion to help towards a re-unification of everything that has ever split off."[156]

Law of Consciousness reflects Experience

"Working out of abundance, produces abundance, but working out of poverty and need, produces more poverty and need."[157]

Law of Fully Inhabiting a State of Consciousness in order to Grow

"You have to reach a certain state, and fully be in that state before it can be abandoned for a further state. It is often overlooked, and even more often, totally ignored.

This is one of the great important laws for man to know and deeply comprehend."[158]

Law of the necessity of independent selection and recognition

"Development means independence, selecting truth from un-truth...you have to learn to distinguish right from wrong, between truth and untruth by truth's own merit and not because...(said by) an authority and therefore it is easy to believe."[159]

Law of Energy used for Spiritually Positive Goals is Always Replenished

"This is why so often people who do a lot of good seem to have su-perhuman strength. Therefore, he who knows what this life is all about will channel wisely the energy at his disposal and flip the switches ac-cordingly. When one just drifts along, without giving a thought to the

156. Pathwork Lecture #193, "Resume of the Basic Principles of the Pathwork, Aim & Process"

157. Pathwork Lecture #132, "Function of the Ego in Relationship to the Real Self"

158. Pathwork Lecture #132, "Function of the Ego in Relationship to the Real Self"

159. Pathwork Lecture #30, "Self Will, Pride & Fear"

true meaning of life, much of the energy will go into false channels and thus be used up without being sufficiently renewed."[160]

Law of Mutuality

"Mutuality is a cosmic or spiritual law. No creation can take place unless mutuality exists. Mutuality means that two apparently or superficially different, or alien, entities or aspects move toward one another for the purpose of uniting and making one comprehensive whole. They open up toward one another, they cooperate with and affect one another, so as to create a new divine manifestation, in whatever form this may be. New forms of self-expression can only come into being when the self merges with something beyond itself. Wherever there is separation, mutuality must prevail, or come into being, in order to eliminate this separation.

Nothing can be created unless mutuality exists, whether it be a new galaxy, a work of art, or a good relationship between human beings. This applies even to the creation of the simplest object.

For mutuality to take place there must be an expansive movement toward this other attitude, aspect, or person. In other words, there must be two expansive movements flowing out toward one another in an harmonious interplay of giving and receiving, of mutual cooperation, of positive opening. To put it differently, two yes-currents must move toward each other."[161]

Law of Help from the World of God

"...it is according to universal law that man himself has to make the first step in order to receive help from the World of God."[162]

---

160. Pathwork Lecture #3, "Choosing Your Destiny—The Will to Change"
161. Pathwork Lecture #185, "Mutuality, A Cosmic Principle & Law"
162. Pathwork Lecture #21, "The Fall"

Law of Free Will

"…one of the most important divine aspects is free will and liberty of choice…God gives the freedom of choice and this has deeper significance than most of you realize. With that freedom, the possibility to abuse the power given and to use it contrary to divine laws, must perforce exist. If no choice were available, there would be no freedom and no power. There can be no divine happiness, in fact, no divinity at all, if it cannot be attained or maintained in free choice. By the same token, the opposite of God and His laws must, of course, be the prohibiting of such free choice and the domination of the stronger over the weaker ones."

"If He would use His infinite power by overruling the free will and the choice of those who decided to use the given power in their own way, He would actually do in principle the same as Lucifer. … for only by remaining true to Himself and His laws would there be a fundamental difference between the ways of God and the ways of Lucifer. Since it is the plan of God that every creature should at one time come back to Him out of free choice and recognition and re- attain divinity, it was imperative that He would not use the same means of force as His opponent, even though the purpose might be a good one.""…means had to be found so that those creatures who desired to return to God and to keep His laws instead of the luciferic ones, could do so within the framework of the laws of God. Thus the free will of no one would be broken, not even of Lucifer himself. This is the great Plan of Salvation, in which Christ played a major role."[163]

Law of Giving Up what you want to Receive

"You know the Spiritual Law: first, you have to give up what you want to gain! You have given up admiration which means you have given up making an impression. You have given up wanting love from others by appearing so wonderful and instead you have made a gift to others by diminishing their loneliness in their supposed imperfection…you have given up your vanity. You have given up some of your Ego. And this is why you must receive in this way, and in this way

---

163. Pathwork Lecture #21, "The Fall"

alone, what you have never succeeded in receiving the other way; your Lower Self has chosen so far in its blindness. If you give up yourself in this way, you bestow the greatest gift you can possibly give to another human being—and therefore, the Law must take effect."[164]

Law of Giving & Receiving

"Let each and every one of you now think about what particular blessings you have: it may be good health, or spiritual strength, or the happiness and security of a loving relationship; it is different with each one of you. Everybody has received a special treasure from God. And once you have made the decision: "I will no longer want to be the ultimate goal, but rather a link in the chain," it will be shown to you how you can pass on that which you have received, and you will also be richly rewarde d, for that is the law."[165]

Law of Inner & Outer Freedom

"...the same law applies here also (law of giving and receiving) :he who desires freedom for selfish reasons will find himself bound on the inner level. On the other hand, he who desires freedom to be a link in the chain, to effect some special task for God's plan of salvation and for his fellow human beings will blossom in his freedom without being bound inside...When he gives his energy to further the upward development of human consciousness, he will be free not only on the outer level, but inwardly also."[166]

---

164. Pathwork Lecture #17, "The Call"

165. Pathwork Lecture #5, "Happiness for Yourself vs. Happiness as a Link in the Chain of Life"

166. Pathwork Lecture #5, "Happiness for Yourself vs. Happiness as a Link in the Chain of Life"

Do Unto Others *(The words of Jesus)*

"Therefore all things whatsoever ye would that men should do to you, do ye even so to them; for this is the law and the prophets."[167]

The Great Commandment:

"Then one of them, which was a lawyer, asked him a question, tempting him, and saying, Master, which is the great commandment in the law: Jesus said unto him, Thou shalt love the lord thy God with all they heart, and with all they soul, and with all they mind. This is the first and great commandment. And the second is like unto it, Thou shalt love thy neighbor as thyself. *On these two commandments hang all the law* and the prophets."[168]

---

167. Matthew 7:12 (KJV)
168. Matthew 22: 35-40 (KJV)

Processes

Finding Your Center

Close your eyes, straighten your back and with gentle intention open your crown and base chakras to the Divine flow of light. Visualize a column of white light rising up from your crown and penetrating the vibratory levels until it reaches the Heart of God.[169] With your awareness, follow that white column down in through your crown, through the center of your chakras, out your base chakra and down into the center of the earth. Anchor your energy there. With your awareness, come up the column into your body, and come to rest in your heart.

Bring your attention to the ball of light, "home base," deep in your heart chakra. Breathe it. Let yourself put down for a moment all your concerns and but's, and just let this moment in time be ok, and let yourself be ok in it. This is your Center of Wisdom and Love.

Repeat daily for the rest of your life. Do it when you're feeling challenged. Do it when you're walking in the woods, at the opera, at a Little League game. It will help you remember who you are.

That's all there is to it. It's not fast and cheap with flashing lights and loud noise. It's not the adrenaline rush of the coffee, sugar, alcohol, control or aggression. It's just now. It's qualities are peace, relaxation, acceptance, joy—all qualities that are enduring—yours alone, and yours that you experience along with everyone else. You enter a vibrational reality that is already inhabited by many—and so few. You're taking the next vital step to arriving home. And, of course, we never "arrive," and we're always arriving.

Come back to "Center" again and again until you live most of your life there.

---

169. High vibratory levels are above us, inside us and all around us.

"A new moon teaches gradualness and deliberation and how one gives birth to oneself slowly. Patience with small details makes perfect a large work, like the universe. What nine months of attention does for an embryo forty early mornings will do for your gradually growing wholeness."

RUMI

WORKING WITH EMOTIONS

Emotions are from the past.
Feelings are flowing and appropriate to the moment

Some guidelines:

- emotions need to be felt and not pushed down
- negative emotions are never acted out on others
- often we are not aware of negative emotions (like hostility or hatred)
- to live fully and feel the pleasure of harmony, emotions need to be moving.
- when we fear our negative emotions and stay hyper alert so we can squash the "wrong" one, we expend a great deal of energy and our capacity to love diminishes. When we're ashamed of our hate and hostility, vindictiveness and envy, we push them down out of our consciousness, thereby they remain strong. These "unacceptable" emotions must be faced and owned, and their root cause understood. If they remain below our "radar" they come out indirectly and compromise our creativity, our ability to have "real" relationships and our fulfillment.
- when the emotions are immature (not faced and understood, rationalized, stuck in the wounded child) they bring unhappiness. We, therefore, unconsciously "protect" ourselves by keeping them buried. We become numb to the "highs" and "lows." And, when we allow this to go on, we experience unhappiness anyway and we get hurt anyway. And, we carry a subconscious

sense of the lack of fullness of a life not complete. When we withdraw from pain, we also withdraw from happiness.

What to do:
— when expressing emotions, always create a sacred space[170]
— look beneath the surface awareness to the subtle emotional currents—intend to connect with the objective part of you that can hold compassion as the place from which you perceive yourself and life
— open to the possibility that you have both positive and negative emotions buried in your unconscious
— start with the areas of disharmony in your life. Ask yourself some probing questions, "Is there a "should" here?" ("should" is often a forcing, parental word) "Do I want to push the other from my self-will?" "Am I afraid to make a mistake?" "What is hurtful to me?" "Is my relationship unfulfilling?" Add more of your own.
— observe your emotions, without judgment—we're dulled to a great extent to what we're feeling. We have to learn to differentiate between a thought and an emotion.
— translate your emotions into words
— look for patterns in your emotional reactions
— keep reminding yourself that your emotions do not define who you are or what your experience is—emotions lie, feelings don't lie
— know what your defenses[171] are. No longer condone the acting out on others of the defensive postures and the negativity that is attached to them.
— understand that certain unacceptable emotions are repressed in the wounded child: anger, resentment, hurt, hate. As long as we don't bring them up into our awareness for what they really are (and not gloss over them as being "caused" by some-

---

170. See Glossary, Sacred Circle
171. See Offense/Defense

one), they cannot heal and we will stay the child and be unable to enter emotional maturity.

In ordinary life, only in extreme crisis do the repressed emotions come to the surface. The crisis is actually caused by the hidden emotional immaturity.

Certain people or situations in our life will touch that place that had the original trauma or that experienced a toxic emotional climate, and the immature emotions will come up.

— be willing to experience your repressed pain

— be willing to experience your aggressiveness and hostility and ask yourself if there is hurt and rejection underneath

— allow the healthy expression of negative emotions[172] in a sacred space with the intention of healing—not for rationalizations or to punish. Try to get down to the naked hatred, the destroyer—this will take you to the deep belly sobbing of the pain of the wound. Going through this process is how emotions can mature.

— notice if you dramatize your emotions, make them bigger; and/or whether you hold back their full force.

The dramatization comes from unrecognized needs, causing a build-up, accompanied by the mistaken belief that the strong emotions will get the need gratified. This is often about what you think another person should feel or do, which tries to force and manipulate others to your will.

The other pole, the fearful repression, causes a shallow life.

Be aware that sometimes emotions are influenced by entities.[173] When you have negative thoughts/emotions, you draw like energies which enhance what is already in you.

— notice if you substitute other emotions for the unacceptable ones.

— be willing to let go of the need to be perfect—look for your humility.

---

172. See Processes: Working with Anger, A Process for Moving Anger

173. See Processes, Working with Entities

— notice how you "feel" about being perfect, having a perfect life and dealing with imperfect situations.

From the mind, we "know" that perfection on this plane is impossible, but emotionally this is not so. We carry fears in the wounded child about not being perfect, therefore not being loved.

We have the deep belief about relationship, that if the other isn't perfect, I cannot be happy.

Notice that you're afraid of being found out, and that you expend a great deal of energy pretending and guarding against exposure.

Unconsciously, we expect complete perfection and we're steeped in duality about it—"Either I'm perfect or I'm un-acceptable." We need to open to the fact that evolving is a process—acceptance, acceptance, acceptance.

Notice if there is shame about not being perfect, and there-fore pretence. Where there is the one, there is the other. And, where there is shame and pretence, there is a fierce pride.

— open to the recognition that the painful emotions are illu-sion
— be open to the realization that the issues in the emotional body are a manifestation of issues with life/God at the soul level
— find your Real Feelings. You can only tell the difference be-tween emotions from defense and Real Feelings when you have observed, understood and worked with releasing your emotional reactions. For a while it will be confusing, then you will begin to recognize what your true feelings are.
— know that you have been programmed to hide, manipulate and use your emotions to get what you "need."
— healing the emotions is the crux of our inner work.
— be willing to hold yourself with compassion
— healthy feeling experience is always moving—God moves.

Ponder this information and use "A Process for Moving Anger" under "Working with Anger" and "Healing Habitual Patterns—The

Signal" and "Healing the Child" under The Format for Healing" as needed for expressing and healing emotions.

> *"Any path of self-realization must deal with the most*
> *subtle, unconscious soul movements and attitudes*
> *because their effect is so much greater than most*
> *individuals only remotely sense.*[174]*"*

A Process for Exploring Sexual Fantasies

Sit with each of these questions in your meditation. Write the Answers; that will make the process more concrete.
*   What is erotic to you?
*   What is the theme of the fantasies?
*   What is the belief behind the fantasy?
*   How does this show up in my life?
Example:
What is erotic? The big, strong man that doesn't show feelings.
Ongoing theme: being overpowered
Belief: I am weak—pleasure connected with being weak.
Outer problem: Need to be taken care of—don't take responsibility.

Working with Anger

When I look at anger being acted out, either mine or someone else's, I see it as fireballs being thrown at a target. You might try remembering your angriest moment. Imagine what the energy looked like, or felt like, as you sent it to someone, or as it came to you. We're generally not conscious of this part. We're too caught up in the fight.

We need to start seeing clearly what we're doing, and what's happening to others. When all is said and done, the *reasons why* we do

---

174. Pathwork Lecture #150, "Self Liking, Condition For Universal State of Bliss"

what we do don't matter. What matters is what we do with our energy. As I'm sure I've said many times in this book, reasons are the "booby" prize. The best part of us knows we don't want to harm anyone. So, we need to be clear that *no one makes you angry*. You make yourself angry. Your anger is yours.

It's very revealing in looking at our anger, to *translate it into words*. It may translate into "I hate you," "I want to kill you," "I want to slap some sense into you." This is a part we've been covering over, losing touch with ourselves and what we are in fact doing. We end up not taking responsibility for our emotions while we take out our sword and slash and stab the other. The darkest part of us has, in fact, been using the other person's faults as a crucible on which to act out our negativity. We cover our tracks, unconsciously, by putting the focus on how wrong the other is, and often they will let you do it because they feel wrong and guilty, anyway. Or, they may take out their sword too and rationalize slashing and stabbing you by the fact that you attacked them and you deserve it. So, it goes on, and on, and on, until we stop it. We stop it, not by stuffing[175] our anger, but by allowing ourselves to feel it, seeing it for what it really is, both our choice to inflict damage and a cover up for our pain. Under our anger, we are hurt (now and in the past). Inside every dragon is a crying child.

Doing this work requires that we deal with our frustration and anger in a positive way. *It is never ok to act it out.* If we stop throwing it at each other, though, what do we do with it? First, we don't want to suppress anything. We're aiming for a positive model of holding a flowing and open state and tolerating our uncomfortable emotions. This is the adult emotional state of being. The adult recognizes that our negative emotions will not swallow us up if we fully acknowledge their presence. At this point in our evolvement, we stop using them to punish. We become aware of the difference between *feeling* angry and *being* angry. The positive model here is the intention to be kind and loving. This doesn't mean that we can't draw a boundary. Love is enormously strong and can say "no" with compassion. (There is a common misconception that if I am loving, I have to let people act out their negativity on me, or I'm weak). We're not taught how to contain our

---

175. See Glossary

lower impulses from our heart, however. The mass consciousness says its right and good to return fire with fire.

We are human and sometimes our negative emotions spill over. It's not that we should "beat ourselves up" when this happens, but rather have compassion for ourselves and know that we're not perfect, but an *evolving* being. The key here, however, is to *know* that you have transgressed and to make amends. (This can easily be misused too, to do whatever you please and then, say an insincere "sorry," thereby not taking true responsibility). We need to be honest with ourselves about what we're feeling.

There is also healthy anger. Healthy anger is necessary. Trying to deny this emotion leads to self-deception about what is healthy anger and what is unhealthy. Also, sometimes when the situation may justify healthy anger, we go into the unhealthy kind and "act out" from our wounding and defense.

We may also fear our anger. We're afraid that even justified anger will take us over and lead us into physical violence. That's why it's so important to allow ourselves to feel our anger consciously. If we don't, we're more likely to erupt verbally and/or physically. When we're fully in touch with justified anger, we don't go into destructive acting out, we're able to tolerate the emotion and stay centered in our love and exactly what action is required under the circumstances. The ability to feel and express our love and our anger are connected. I have to say, however, that until the wells of suppressed anger and rage are cleared out, we can't be objective about what is justified and what is not. We can easily misuse the concept of justified anger to rationalize acting out.

We're not taught healthy expression of our anger or what to do when anger is "thrown" at us. When someone comes at us with smoking pistols, we must draw a boundary. First and foremost, the heart can say no.

When you get charged, it's appropriate to say something like, "I'm angry right now, give me a few minutes. Then, you go inside and look for what in the past was catalyzed by the present.[176] Forget about what the other guy did. The solution to the issue and your healing are in-

---

176. See Format for Healing

side yourself. Your charge is from your past, not with the person across from you. If you didn't have a wound, you would know that their transgression was from their wounding—they're aggressive because they're afraid of feeling helpless; they're withdrawing because they're afraid of getting hurt; they're sucking your energy because they believe they don't have what you have.

Although we try to do the right thing and take the high road of loving kindness, we're human and imperfect and frustrations and anger can build up inside us. We can hold it in to such a degree that we walk around simmering a lot of the time; short-tempered and punishing to whomever crosses our path. Or, we push the anger down—into our bodies and unconscious mind—and lose touch with the fact that it's there. In this case, anger can erupt and go out of control. We can flail out at others or turn it inward, punishing ourselves and/or making ourselves physically and /or mentally sick.

One area where many of us are reluctant to go is the anger we have at our parents. We've all been wounded by our parents—that's an integral part of the process of incarnation—and, while there's pain in the wounding, we're also angry with what they did/said. In order to *fully experience the wounding of our childhood*, we must allow ourselves to feel all the hurt and pain, even though our Higher Self knows they did the best they could. We have to express it and learn from it. It happened because our soul has lessons to learn.

As we delve into these deep places, intention is everything. Intending to get in touch and express for healing is a high vibration. Expressing to indulge the anger is a low vibration and accomplishes nothing except to take us into more negativity.

Because of our conditioning, we *hold negative emotions as unacceptable*. We suppress them, rationalize them and deny them. We're terrified that if they come up we'll lose the love that we need so desperately. When we suppress our negativity, it in fact comes out anyway. It slides out under our radar.

The following are some signals that we may be leaking anger:[177]
- Procrastination
- Lateness

---

177. No source listed

- Sarcastic or ironic humor
- Cynicism or flippancy
- Over-politeness, constant cheerfulness, attitude of "grin and bear it."
- Frequent sighing
- Smiling while hurting
- Over-controlled, monotone speaking voice
- Frequent disturbing or frightening dreams
- Difficulty sleeping
- Boredom, apathy, loss of interest
- Exaggerated slowing down of movements
- Getting tired more easily than usual
- Chronic irritability
- Consistent drowsiness
- Excessive sleeping
- Waking up tired
- Clenched jaws/teeth grinding—especially while sleeping
- Any unconsciously repeated physical movement
- Chronically stiff or sore neck
- Chronic depression
- Stomach problems

A process for moving anger:

Use your intention to *create a sacred space,*[178] ask for help from your guides and whatever other light beings you feel connected to. Ask that the negative energy harm no one and be removed for transformation.

Go inside and look for what is present. It may help to replay the scenario that triggered you. As the emotion comes fully to the surface, let go of the scenario and focus on the emotion. Allow the anger to come up fully.

You can *release* by hitting, screaming or by giving your energy to the earth (touching a tree or the ground). The earth will purify your

---

178. See Glossary, Sacred Circle

negative energy. You can visualize it moving out your base chakra and the small charkas in the soles of your feet.

If it feels best to let your emotions out physically, you can hit your bed with your fists (by standing with your knees slightly bent, feet shoulder width apart, and bringing your fists over your head and directly down, hard). While doing this, make a deep, guttural sound in your throat. (We have "swallowed" a lot) You can also use a tennis racket or encounter bat. Another way to release is to scream in your car or into a pillow. Really let it rip! Remind yourself to stay present and connected. (That is, fully present in your mind, body and emotions) You don't want to disconnect and go on automatic. If it's difficult for you to bring it out, you may need to "act as if" for a few minutes until you connect. If you get angry a lot, be careful not to "loop."[179] If you have trouble getting angry, or if you feel shaky about releasing emotions, it may be best to work with someone whom does emotional release work.[180] As you are working with the anger, at the plateaus, ask your Wisdom what the anger is saying. Try not to edit. We don't like to see ourselves as negative people, so it may be difficult to let yourself know what the statement is. But for the sake of your healing, persevere.

Often, as we release to the fullest the energy burst of the anger, spontaneous tears will come. Deep belly sobbing is the core release. It's the connection to the pain of the wound. It's what is under the anger—the pain of the child/soul. Allow the tears to run their course. You may spontaneously know what you are crying about, if not, then wait until you reach a plateau before you go on. As the emotions level off, see if you can decode the tears—what are they saying? And, here we find the root of the problem. We have been wounded and out of this wounding came a wrong belief about a parent, therefore every man and/or every woman—and about life/God. Out of this belief, we create the same experience over and over, the child trying to get what he/she didn't get from mother or father. We paste the past onto

179. See Glossary

180. I recommend a Core Energetic Therapist - www.coreenergeticsinstitute. com

the present. We then cover the pain with aggression/shutting down emotions/manipulation.

These *thoughtforms* of the wrong belief/emotional reaction are energetically around us as a presence in our field that we feed and make stronger every time we think, feel and/or act out of this wrong belief. The thoughtform has a vibration and it attracts the people and circumstances it believes in. Thus, we act out of an automatic habitual process to stimuli from the outside, blindly, thinking we are at choice in our lives when we are really like robots—being impacted, reacting; being impacted, reacting. Until we are willing to face our pain and our darker actions and intents, we won't be able to transform.

Energetically, as we get to the root of our misconception/emotional charge, and we begin to release the pent-up emotions and understand what happened and why, the inverted energy transforms back to its original form—a harmonic. We notice that the emotional release and concurrent understanding has opened the contracted energy and moved it. When our energy moves, it feels good. *What is harmonious is always moving*—God is movement.

As we get through the old pain and realize what has happened and what our teaching is, gratitude arises.

After a while, this process becomes second nature. We create the healing habit of going directly inside when something uncomfortable happens. We do this, not as a neurotic habit or as the vigilante, but as the compassionate nurturer that accepts our mistakes and our forgetting as the medicine for our healing.

We no longer hurt people with our anger, act it out, or deny it, but go into gratitude for the catalyst of our soul's healing. Now, we're "light years" from, "it's your fault," "you're bad and wrong."

For those who "spill over" a lot, it's necessary to learn to contain[181] your energy. If you work with this healing paradigm, and intend to tolerate your emotions, you'll move out of knee-jerk acting out and get to the root of your issue.

For those who repress anger, it's important for your health –mentally, emotionally, physically and spiritually—to open your emotional body. We all have wells of buried emotions from childhood that need

---

181. See Glossary

to be cleared out. When we cut off the unpleasant emotions, we cut off some of the pleasant ones too.

In order to fully inhabit our spirituality, we must have a free-flowing system. How can we fully love if we haven't known hatred? How can we raise our vibration if we haven't transformed our density?

"If you circumambulated every holy shrine in the world
ten times,
it would not get you to heaven
as quick
as controlling your anger."

KABIR

WORKING WITH THE LOWER SELF

As we begin to open these realms, it's necessary to:
— *connect to the Higher Self/Loving Witness/Godman*—this is the consciousness from which we look at darkness
— *the cornerstone, consciously intend to love.*
— be willing to accept that you have darkness
— 99% of the people are not in touch with the fact that they have and act out negative energies
— hold in awareness that you're ultimately looking for the Divine aspect of the negative—every negative energy is the inversion of a Divine energy
— hold in your awareness that you are cause to your own effects
— have the intention to be objective and watch thoughts, emotions, actions, and words.
— cultivate acceptance without judgment
— be willing to *feel* all the way through this process
— know that darkness is only fear, and it is temporary
— know that our negativity is largely unconscious and/or rationalized—we have to look for it in our disharmonic life manifestation, our thoughts, words, and deeds.
— Ask yourself, "what is my part?" in the disharmonies in your life. These situations are the signal (and the manifestation) of

something negative in us. Make a list. This begins to break our conditioning to blame and make it all about the other or circumstances. This is taking deep responsibility for our lives.

— Be willing to tolerate pain—darkness is a defense against pain. Fighting pain on this earth plane is like fighting gravity. It exists and is a part of life. It gives us impetus to grow. By accepting the truth of this, we become softer, more resilient, less defended.

— Make an honest list of your faults. To really be thorough, you might ask your family and friends what your faults are. It's necessary here not to respond, and to notice what comes up in you—excuses, whitewashing, reasons. Be aware that you draw a negative entity for every fault you carry. They will feed off your drama and intense emotions. Their "job" is to keep you right where you are—anti-movement, anti-life.

— Look for your "mask." That is the idealized view you have of yourself that comes from the fear in childhood that you wouldn't be loved unless you were a "certain" way. We're desperately afraid of being revealed for who we think we "really" are—unacceptable. A clue to finding your mask is look for the situations when you *must* been "seen" as intelligent, good looking, successful, etc., or when it's unbearable to be "seen" as inept, stupid, a failure, etc. The mask directs negativity through "socially acceptable" channels. The "mask-self" is a place where it's easy to get caught in projection, self-justification, self-righteous exoneration, blaming, making excuses, self-indulgence, denial, repression, evasion.

— Find your defense.[182] See where negativity attaches to the defense. Find the negative pleasure[183] in your defense.

— Look for your negative intent—when you're about to make a choice about something, ask yourself, "What is my Higher Self intent and lower self intent?"

— Reveal yourself to at least one other human being—ask for help from a teacher and from your spiritual guides. Reveal

---

182. See Offense/Defense

183. See Glossary

your destructiveness, materialism and half-truths with compassion and without judgment.
— Forgive yourself
— Make restitution
— Meditate
— Pray with sincerity
— Remember, the darkness is there to reveal your Divinity.

Our greatest fear is the fear of our own lower self.

"One does not become enlightened by imagining figures of light, but by making the darkness conscious."

CARL JUNG

WORKING WITH ENTITIES

To begin, do your inner work[184] to discover the issue at hand, along with your wound.

As we expand our consciousness, we become aware that we are influenced by beings from other dimensions, both light and dark. Connecting to our Guides for help and other angelic energies from the Christ Consciousness, and releasing dense energies is an integral part of purification work.

As we have discussed, for each area of misconception that we carry, an entity of like vibration is drawn to us. The same is true for the areas of harmony. We're a mixture of different vibratory levels that lives in a universe made up of energy.

Therefore, as we do our inner work, it's very helpful to know that we're being "talked to" and our emotions are being stirred up by negative entities to keep us contracted and small. We become a pawn in the agenda of the dark forces when we choose our defenses and close our hearts. So, as we turn to healing our mental misconceptions and

---

184. See Format for Healing

emotional reactions, we want to dismiss these energies because, of course, they don't want the healing.

To dismiss an entity, we need help. Although we are sovereign of our field, we are not just our conscious mind. Our unconscious sometimes has strong opposition to the process—that is, misconceptions that believe these negative energies are "helping." So, we often need someone in the body present to add their light to ours, to remain objective, to confront a blindness we may have, and to accomplish the release. If you're alone, call a high healer in the Christ Consciousness to assist.

Center[185] yourself and connect with your guides.

Call in Angelic beings that are experts in protection from dark interference. While the highest protection is your sincere heart and your spiritual health, we are also a work in progress.

Next, create a sacred circle and call in help from the angelic kingdom. I call the Archangels (sometimes a specific one "comes to mind"), the Masters, and any high angelic beings in the Christ Consciousness that have expertise in removing dark energies. (I specify "Christ Consciousness" because I want a clear and high circle, and no interference from beings masquerading as light). Ask that the entity be taken back where it came from (we don't want them to attach to someone else with an unconscious resonance). They are from other dimensions and they must be sent back and away from this sphere.

Another area to be aware of is the presence of any discarnate beings—ghosts. There are many around, and often souls that have passed on will stay with a loved one, or someone they have an issue with, for a long time, if not the whole life span. That energy is, for the most part, like having Auntie Grace or perhaps mother sitting there with you. While well meaning, they may interfere with the healing because they may not understand what is happening. They can be quite stubborn, and also you may be attached and not want to let go. Firmly and lovingly ask any discarnate beings to leave until the healing is complete.

When tuning in to the presence of a negative entity, we want to discern the specific consciousness. At its clearest, it will be a state-

---

185. See Processes, Finding Your Center

ment, such as "Life sucks so I drink," or "I'm weak," or "They're all against me," or "I'm better." The statement of the energy may come to you as a thought, a picture on your mind screen, an emotion, and words whispered in your ear, a physical sensation.[186] Whatever you get, follow it by asking questions. We do not interact with an entity or try to bring it to the light. We observe to see what it is, that is all.

As you get ready to release the entity, see if you can find your "need" for it. This will be *emotional logic* connected to the issue and wound. Our conscious logical mind knows that we don't need something negative, but the limited consciousness of the wounded child may be attached to "a drinking buddy," or help making money (an entity of greed).

Bring your awareness to your sovereignty over your body and your field. When you command (not from the wounded ego), the energy will go. As you occupy this consciousness, also be aware of letting go of the misconception that drew the energy in and be willing to let go of any attachment to "help." You don't have to be perfectly free of wanting it, just sincerely willing to let it go. When the entity is gone, you can work much more effectively with the issue at hand.

Stay tuned in and pay attention, and as you work at it, you will get more and more information about these realms. Clear your field (body and aura) regularly.[187]

WORKING WITH MEDITATION

Meditation is essential for spiritual progress. It's a powerful way to connect to the Reality of who you are, train your mind, and detach from the "desire nature."

---

186. See Approaching Healing Energetically
187. See Additional Materials, Energetic Clearing & Protection

I use Vipassana[188] Meditation, which focuses on the breath. The breath is deeply connected to the mind, so by following the breath you calm the mind and learn non-attachment to earthly things. In Vipassana, we also do walking meditation. Generally, the practice is: 45 minutes sitting, 45 minutes conscious walking.

As you sit, keep your back straight and come into the moment. Allow your thoughts to pass by as clouds in the sky. Breathe. Keep bringing your attention back to your breath, having compassion for the "runaway mind." Even when your mind is active during a sitting, you are receiving benefit.

You might start with 10 or 20 minutes morning and night, even 5 minutes—but it is important to start.

I have done meditation retreats for many years, and find that they are one of the best gifts I give to myself.

"Be still and know that I am God"[189]

---

188. There is much literature, tapes, etc., and many places to do retreats and get teachings.

    The magazine, Shambhala Sun is a great resource for information as well as beautiful teachings. Shambhala Sun, 1345 Spruce Street, Boulder, CO 80302-4886. The following are Vipassana retreat centers: Insight Meditation Society, in Barre, Massachusetts, and Spirit Rock Meditation Center, PO Box 169, Woodacre, California, 94973, www.spiritrock.org.

189. Psalms 46:8

Glossary

Adult - God Consciousness: the mature ego consciousness infused with the love of spirit. The adult aspect is a mature, wise, kind consciousness that can handle the things of the world. This is the healthy third chakra. This mature being directs the healthy ego toward spirit. As it penetrates the levels of spirit, it becomes harmonized with, and the vehicle for, love.

Aikido: a Japanese martial art that uses the principle of joining with the attack of the opponent, rather than meeting force with force. By moving with the attacker the defender may redirect the attacker's momentum with small effort…Aikido is often translated as "the Way of unifying with life energy" or as "the Way of harmonious spirit. The goal in developing this martial art was to create an art practitioners could use to defend themselves while also protecting the attacker from injury.[190]

When I speak of using aikido in purification work, I mean using the momentum of the negative energy as a signal to move into healing.

Archetypes: the quintessential characteristics of a particular psychological/emotional pattern. For instance, when we talk about a "nun", we all know the characteristics of this human pattern. Some common archetypes are: king, queen, princess, priest, Madonna, whore, slave, holy man, knight, gigolo, rich businessman, hippie, nerd, model. We often identify unconsciously with one or more archetype.

Astral Plane: a ring of energy around the planet filled with everything we know, or have ever imagined. The energies in the astral run the gamut from dark to light—angels to devils. Disembodied souls often get caught in the astral by their unresolved emotional is-

---

190. Definition from "Wikipedia" <http://www.wikipedia.com.

sues. Some disciplines refer to the emotional level of the aura as the astral.

Charged: an experience whereby we're full of emotion in reaction to something in the present that triggers a connection to an unresolved issue in the past.

Child Consciousness: the wounded child consciousness is the state that is fearful, angry, unworthy and self-centered that holds the world as a limited, unsafe place. This kind of consciousness makes generalizations about situations and people (if Mom is invasive, all women are invasive). The healthy child consciousness is the home of spontaneity, creativity, a sense of self that is secure and knows it's a part of everything, intuition.

"There is a difference between childishness and childlikeness. Childishness means immaturity. Childlikeness does not mean immaturity at all; it can be very mature. Childishness means distortion, ignorance, limitation, helplessness, dependency, with the inevitable selfishness and self-centeredness attached to these trends. Childlikeness means being an unwritten leaf—which the most mature person can be, in the sense of approaching each situation with a newness and freshness, without preconceived ideas, prejudice, ready-made concepts. It approaches all of life with a keener sense of experiencing— typical of a child whose senses are not dulled by paralyzing defenses. Most older people, because they are tired and disillusioned, lack the spirit of adventure and courage to be found in children. But this is not an inevitable result of age, it is a result of prejudice, superstition, limitation in concept and outlook and emotional and mental distortions. The qualities of childlikeness are an inevitable result of spiritual maturity, when this childlikeness replaces childishness."[191]

Childhood Wounding: As a part of our incarnational process, we come into a family that will catalyze our soul's misunderstandings about the nature of the universe/God. We experience the emotions of our misconception so that we can "remember" mentally, physically,

---

191. Pathwork Manuscript of Eva Pierrakos: *Path to the Real Self, Q & A*

emotionally and spiritually, the Truth of the Divine. We heal our wounded child through re-parenting from the "good parent" at the psychological level, and the Godwoman/man at the spiritual level.

Christ Consciousness: Pure, Unconditional Love

Confrontation: This process is not primarily to resolve anything with the other person, or to change them, but an attempt to get closer.

When we're dealing with a disharmony with the other, and *after we have done our own work*, there are times when it's appropriate to confront an energy in the other. This is not a license to blame, but rather an attempt at intimacy. If you can find the place inside you that truly wants to get closer to this person, you can say what you think you see and how you react to it. Describing your energies is to reveal yourself and be vulnerable[3]. It doesn't hold an expectation that the other person is supposed to take care of your wounded child.

It is, of course, possible they will be angry and defensive. This has to be ok with you. Not that you allow someone to act out negatively on you, but that you have no demands on them. Sometimes, the other person is not willing, at this time, to look at this particular energy. This doesn't mean that you're better or necessarily more evolved. You may be ready to deal with healing certain energy now and they are not, and they may be ready to face certain energies in themselves that you are not. We can never compare.

It's indulging in negativity to make someone bad and wrong. Sometimes, we try to use non-blaming language in an attempt to cover our judgment, but it still comes out, "I feel that you are being cruel." We've got the "I feel" right, because we want to be talking about ourselves; but in the example you're still making an *evaluation* of someone's behavior. So, you want to say something like, "When you said, "_____," I felt hurt. Most people will not do any self-examination around it, but will say something like, "I didn't mean to hurt you." Which often translates into, "What's wrong with you that you got hurt by that?" However, the confrontation is a way to establish boundaries, help the other person to understand you, it's a lesson in patience and compassion, and it breaks down the barriers of separation. There's a place here where the unhealed ego might come in with how much better you are because you're more aware, but this can be another spiritual practice in humility—some wonderful people are still asleep in certain areas. When you've had many experiences with people who don't take responsibility for their energies, you'll meet one who does, and you'll know the power that one person can have.

Our focus needs to be on doing the right thing because it's the right thing and not because of what others will think of us, or to aggrandize ourselves. The purpose of the friction is for us to do our inner healing, not to appear "cool" or remake someone else so they don't do or say things that upset us.

In general, if this other person is someone who is likely to react negatively and only wants to fight, then we have to ask ourselves if we want this kind of energy in our life.

On the other hand, in general, if the person can "meet" you by listening with sincerity, you have the basis for some deep relating—actually, you've found a precious jewel.

Contain: The ability to contain is holding a part of us from the vantage point of the Loving Witness; where we feel all our feelings, think all our thoughts, watch our actions and are at the point where we can choose which ones we're going to give our attention and energy to.

We also sometimes need to contain—in the sense of "reign in"—our emotions, thoughts, words or actions because we have a tendency to spill over. Containing ourselves in this way from compassion is a process of restoring balance, inside and out.

Contraction: A contracted energy is tight and unmoving. Any thought or emotion that comes from a disharmonic belief shows up in your field as a dark or muddied color, and has a static form. Any energy that is disharmonic and static is painful. As the energy (and the misconception and emotional charge) is explored for healing, it opens, the emotions move, and we discover what's at the root, that is, the belief that caused the mind, emotions and energy to contract in fear.

If you look at contraction psychologically, it shows up as rigid beliefs with no willingness to explore alternatives. If you look at contracted emotions, they would show up as emotions stuck in a pattern that repeats and repeats. They're not congruent with thoughts and actions, and are out of proportion and inappropriate to the situation.

Cords: Energetic cords are the energy of thoughts and emotions, which become cord-like forms that are sent to someone to pull energy. For instance, if you feel as though you must have a certain person in your life to take care of you (physically and/or emotionally), because they have something you don't, you may unconsciously send a cord to their third chakra (or second or first; or perhaps the kidneys, heart) and pull their energy into you. The receptor site of the person corded may hold the belief that "I am supposed to take care of others, even to my own detriment, that is the way life is." Or, "I'll let you have my energy so you'll love me." You can "cut" cords with your intention.[192]

Defense System: The stance toward life that copes with the wounds of childhood. There are as many ways to look at defense systems, as there are therapies. A simple, and very effective, definition is the existence of three essence energies of God that are twisted and misused for pseudo-protection: Love, Wisdom and Power. Love misused as an imbalance of emotion and the need to be loved by everyone all the time; Wisdom misused as objectivity without feeling; Power misused is aggression.

Alice A. Bailey calls these energies the "three major rays."[193] The Pathwork guide describes them as Divine Attributes with corresponding defense systems.[194]

Devas: "...the angel or deva kingdom...The blending of the deva or angel evolution and the human. This is a mystery which will be

---

192. See Additional Materials, "Energetic Clearing and Protection."

193. Bailey, Alice A., *Esoteric Healing, Volume IV, A Treatise on the Seven Rays,* 10th Printing (New York: Lucis Publishing Company, 1980).

194. Pathwork Lecture #84, "Love, Power and Serenity as Divine Attributes and as Distortions."

solved as man arrives at the consciousness of his own solar Angel...
The angel or deva evolution is one of the great lines of force[195]...

"...the deva lives which build the forms indwelt by all the Sons of God, they know not pain or loss or poverty[196]...

The lowest types of devas or builders on the evolutionary Path are violet devas; next come the green, and last of all, the white devas. These are all dominated by a fourth and special group. These control the exoteric processes of physical plane existence[197]...humans who are a the stage of "...only sensing the inner truth...are aided by hands of...the blue and rose." (Others) "...who suggest, guide and control. Great white and gold devas attend their labours...Back again of these three groups stand the Masters and the devas of the formless levels— a Great Brotherhood, pledged to serve humanity.[198]

Emotional Reaction: An uncomfortable and 'unacceptable' emotion connected to an unresolved issue in our past, from which we react from our defense. Emotional reactions are not appropriate to the situation in the now. They are our signal that we are in illusion.

Emotional Reality: Emotional reality is the consciousness of our emotions, which is generally at odds with our mental reality. We decode our emotions by translating them into statements. For example, anger might say, "I want to kill you." Tears may say, "Poor me," or "There is only pain." Also, the emotional beliefs of the wounded child that may not agree with our rational adult beliefs or spiritual beliefs cause us much pain and discomfort. For example, my spiritual belief may be that the Godforce is loving, but my wounded child may believe that the male Godforce (father) abuses—therefore, all men abuse. Our adult/spiritual self will unconsciously act out the emotional beliefs of the child. (To the child, father is the stand-in for the male aspect of God and mother is the stand-in for the female aspect

195. Bailey, Alice A., *A Treatise on White Magic or The Way of the Disciple*, 17th Printing (New York: Lucis Publishing Company, 1934) 100, 101.

196. Ibid, p532.

197. Ibid, p. 389.

198. Ibid, p354.

of God). These beliefs from our wounding lead directly to our soul's teaching.[199]

Energy Leak: This is a flow of energy out of the body/aura that depletes the life force.

Energetic Signature: The sum total of different vibratory levels. This sum total is the energetic signature of our thoughts and emotions, conscious and unconscious, positive and negative.

Experts: This refers to a realm of darkness that contains those beings that specialize in influencing humanity in ways specific to man's faults, i.e., if you have the fault of jealousy, you will draw an entity that is an expert in influencing you to think jealous thoughts, feel jealous feelings and act in jealous ways.

Field: When I speak of our field, I mean our body and the layers of the aura.

Forcing Current: this is an energy that is a demand and wants to push to get what it wants. It comes from repressed needs. There is an urgency and compulsive quality to it.

Forgetting: Our soul's journey into the many, many experiences of the cosmos has resulted in a "forgetting" of certain true essences of the universe: omnipresence, abundance, connection, etc. This "forgetting" produces pain. Our healing process in this "school" of human experience is when all is said and done, "remembering" that all is love.

Frustration: a forcing current that wants to extract from life the desires of the "little self".
We can work with this forcing current by:
recognizing that when we're frustrated we're in a contracted state.
connecting with our Real Self/Higher Self and finding a place

---

199. See Format for Healing

that is willing to give up self-will; recognizing that not getting what you desire is not a tragedy.

Allowing the possibility that some good can come from it.

Looking for your lesson—what could this be teaching me?

Opening to the expansion of letting go of the tightness against life.

As long as you experience frustration, there is a teaching for you.

God, Names: Some names of God: Aramaic—the language Jesus spoke: Awoon (pronounced ab-woon—the vowel opens the crown and the consonants carry the energy down through your being), Latin: Deus, Arabic: Allah, Christian: God, Lord, Jehovah. Some spiritual teachers say that the ancient languages hold the energy of the words much more than modern languages. It is a wonderful spiritual practice to chant a name of God silently whenever you think of it.

Guidance: When our extrasensory perception opens, we begin to hear, see, or feel guidance from our personal teachers. The teachings and help can come in through our thoughts, we may hear through our physical ears, we may see them clairvoyantly, and we may feel certain bodily sensations or emotions. Usually there is more than one guide, and they come closer to us the more we purify. They will not only teach us spiritual truths but will help with all the mundane life situations. We need to listen carefully and learn to discern what is light as opposed to dark masquerading as light. (A good method is simply to ask, "Are you in the Christ Consciousness?"—Contracted energies will appeal to the unhealed ego: our pride, fear, greed, selfishness, etc.)

Harmony: Energy and consciousness that is aligned with love. When we're aligned with love, our energy is moving and we're happy and at peace. When energy is not in a loving state—disharmony—there is conflict and pain.

Higher Self: This is the consciousness that recognizes that all is well and the universe loves. It's not that this level does not see darkness, but it's not affected negatively by it. This level of consciousness holds deep compassion, is calm, kind, loving, centered, powerful and wise. This is the Real Self, and this real self gradually becomes self-less.

(Synonyms in this text: Essence, Center, Divine Self, Loving Witness, and Inner Guide)

Humanity: With this word I mean the part of the ego that is in misconception and is attached to the 3-D. It's attached and identified with the physical, mental and emotional experience as real.

There is also an aspect of our humanity that we carry in a healthy way as "humanity consciousness." It's the part of us that experiences life as a human and is affected by it, even though we carry a deep spiritual identity. For example we cannot deny the human part of us that misses the physical contact of someone who has crossed over and left the physical body, even though we may know deeply and clearly that death is only a transition to another dimension. The spiritual cannot deny the human. We are both. The spiritual in us can, however, embrace, accept and have compassion for the human. It's our human experience that helps us to "know" what others are going through—a basis for compassion.

Idealized Self: that made-up "picture" we have of ourselves as perfect, good, smart, loving, etc., that is rooted in our childhood need to be loved. See Mask.

Identify: think of ourselves in a certain way, for instance, if I identify with my inner child, I think that the thoughts and emotions of the child are "me."

Imagination: The imagination has a negative connotation in our society. And, it can be used as an escape, which is a choice not to be in life. However, the positive use of the imagination can be to bridge into clairvoyance. With our imagination and our intention we can move energy, we can imagine what an energy might look like. Before long, we will "see" it on our mind screen.

Initiation: As we evolve into greater and greater levels of harmony, we pass through stages of development. As we enter each stage, our energy comes into more alignment and we let go of the dense energy of misconceptions that have been healed. These are stages of initiation[200] into light.

Inner Guide: the part of us that we go to for wisdom. When we're not yet awake to the inner, the guide is our conscience. As we turn inside, the awareness of complexity of the self increases (higher self, lower self, mask self, sub-personalities, archetypes) and our intention to go to the deepest and best in us moves into the first stages of the compassionate witness. This compassionately objective stage begins to witness the outer self; thoughts, emotions, words, actions. As one moves through the spectrum of awakening and healing, the Loving Witness continues to deepen until it experiences life as seeing, feeling, knowing, and hearing only love. The healed ego connecting to the Divine becomes the vehicle for love.

(Synonyms in this text are: Higher Self, Center, Loving Witness, Essence, Divine Self)

Judgment: Discerning that attaches a value of good, bad, right or wrong.

Leaking Energy: When we lose life force because we have an inability to control its flow, and hence cannot use it effectively in the service of the heart.

Little Ego: The limited, wounded, self-interested part of the ego. The "healthy ego" connected to spirit comes in to heal the misconceptions and pain of the little ego.

Looping: This is an emotional state whereby a person gets stuck repeating the same emotion without moving through it to the next stage of healing. It has an empty and compulsive feeling to it.

---

200. For more information, see: Bailey, Alice A., *Initiation, Human and Solar* (New York: Lucis Publishing Company) and other works by Alice Bailey.

Loving Witness: that state of consciousness that is the highest point of loving clarity that we can access. This clarity and compassionate presence is focused on healing what is unhealed, and witnessing the unfolding of our Divine perception. It's our Real Self, (Divine self, Essence, Higher Self, Center, Inner Guide) that is, the state beyond the limited self that has transcended identification with the mind, emotions and body. It's a state that continually deepens as we reach higher and higher vibrations until our consciousness merges with the oneness—and then all evolvement continues. The level of consciousness of our witness is a significant yardstick of our evolvement.

Lower Self: There are two levels of lower self or negative energies that people carry. The more superficial level is the level of negativity. These are energies like blaming, spite, hurtfulness, punishing behaviors, put-downs, and destructiveness to self and others. The deeper level is the *intent* to be negative. For most of us, this level is in the unconscious and we have to dig for it. It's a life-changing experience to find it. Bringing the intent to hurt, destroy, undo, separate, etc., into our conscious mind and emotions removes huge densities from our field, heals unconscious misconceptions about life, frees up our mental and emotional bodies and makes the way for huge bursts of healing and light to come into our field. As long as darkness is hidden, it remains strong.

Maligning: This is talking negatively about someone behind his/her back. Energetically, it is sticking a knife in their back.

Mask: See Idealized Self. We think and act out of our mask self, which often takes the form of ingenuous goodness, lip service loving and rationalized darkness.

Mass Consciousness: The shared ideas of a vast number of people. For instance, large numbers of people agree that fast food is acceptable.

Master: This is a term referring to a state of consciousness that indicates a degree of healthy control and witnessing of self and the world from compassion. It's a state of being that recognizes itself as spirit and an integral part of everything and everyone. It no longer fights, but gives. It sees itself and the world through the eyes of love. It has learned "mastery" of the "little self," the unhealed ego. It perceives and embodies the adaptation of the limited self to the expanded self and the harmony of God that permeates all things.

Merging: On the human level, merging is two autonomous beings choosing to connect, trust, hold each other as precious, and be mutually inter-dependent. Inter-dependence happens when each person has a deep knowing that they can take care of themselves and be either alone or with someone, and they choose to allow the other to do for them as a gift. The barriers of defense are surrendered and you "give over" to love. On the energetic level, you allow your energies to blend with those of the other.

On the Divine level of merging with God, the human level is a pre-requisite. If we can't surrender to another human being, we can't surrender to God. That human being is God, and reflects our Divine relationship. At the spiritual level, we surrender our "no" to love, life, and God. We give up our separateness and bring our uniqueness to take our place in the circle of light.

Negative Pleasure: The child doesn't know the difference between negative and positive. Therefore, whatever the child experiences, negative or positive, it attaches pleasure to it. For example, from the experience of the abusive father we may later be the kind of man you find attractive and exciting; you may become your critical mother and take pleasure in it; the abandoning mother may become the energy in us that creates being "poor abandoned me."

There will also be negative pleasure attached to the defense. The person whose energies are polarized in the mind will feel "good" about their inability to feel. They will also have a sense of superiority—which will feel "good." The person with the aggressive defense will take pleasure in controlling; the person with the submissive defense will take pleasure in manipulating to be taken care of.

Then there is the extreme case of the masochist or sadist who have been wounded to such an extent that they consciously seek out and feel pleasure in emotional and/or physical pain.

Negativity and Negative Intent: Negativity is a superficial layer of the negative that criticizes, maligns, teases with a sting, etc.

Negative intent is the deeper layer of the negative that is "clean" in the sense that it is straight-forward, "I want to hurt you" "I want to kill you" "I hate you." It's not veiled in rationalizations and reasons.

"Off": This is a word used to describe anything that is not in the harmony of love.

Personality: The ego that presents itself to the world. It contains the parts of the ego that are harmonized with love and the unhealed parts. In general, when I refer to the "personality," I mean the unhealed ego.

Polarities: Both ends of a spectrum that we experience like a tennis ball—first one, then the other, or we experience one end of the pole and are not in touch with the other. We are unable to find center. For example, depression then feeling "hi," or binging on food, then denying the self. If we're aware of only one end of a polarity, we must find the other end in us before we can come to center.

Qualities: See Virtues

Reality: Reality with a capital "R"—that is, the Truth that the foundation of the universe is love—the Reality of God.

React: When we think, feel, speak or do from an experience and/or a climate of our childhood.

Receptor Sites: This is the energetic, psycho-emotional place where we hold misconceptions that accept negative energies, for example, "Life is suffering. I'm supposed to suffer." The psycho-emotional aspect shows up as an energy in our field. This energy vibrates at a certain frequency that will draw like-frequencies to it.

Recognition: the full experience of knowing through the body, mind, and emotion and spirit.

Respond: When we think, feel, speak or do in a manner appropriate to the current circumstance without emotional reaction.

Sacred Circle: Creating through your intention a Divine energetic space. It takes two or more, so if you are alone, invite in an angelic presence. This is a circle of energy, created from your intention, for healing, prayer or meditation; and is protected from dark influence.

Self: The conscious awareness of "me," and the unconscious. The self is also the physical, emotional, and expanded energies around the body (the aura).

Soul: the eternal consciousness that travels from lifetime to lifetime healing it's misconceptions about the nature of the Godforce and "remembering" the Truth of God.

Spiritual Practice: a consistent repetition with presence and sincerity of bringing through our body/mind/emotions/spirit a healed pattern—the thought and feeling—that is aligned with light and harmony; a consistent repetition of prayers. (Prayers need to be alive—that is, sincere and in the moment, not by rote).

Stuffing: Pushing our anger and/or pain down below the level of our consciousness where it festers. Since it is denied, it will show up as an eruption. These repressed emotions can also show up as physical disease, such as: arthritis and ulcers are connected to stress; lung disease is connected to grief. There is an emotional connection with every physical disease. The mass consciousness has found only a few.

Subpersonalities: Those split-off, psycho-emotional aspects of ourselves that are in misconception about life/God, for instance, the judge, the critic, the "good" girl/boy, the "bad" girl/boy. The doorway to healing and integrating these energies is to ask ourselves, "Who is speaking?"

Teaching: When I refer to getting "our teaching," I mean the Reality of Love that we are trying to remember at the soul level. We get there through the childhood wounding, which holds the emotional level of the soul's forgetting. For example, if the childhood wound is abandonment, the soul's teaching may be that God is omnipresent.

Third dimension --3-D: When I say 3-D, I mean the reality that we can see, hear and touch physically.

Transmission: The sending of a harmonic energy through embodiment—that is, learning through experience. For instance, if you're with someone who is struggling with the pain of letting go of an addiction, and you've experienced this and come through it to health and peace, you can consciously send the healed paradigm to the person. I feel it in my heart chakra and send it from there. (We do this all the time with each other).

Unitive State: The level of consciousness that has healed the separated ego; that sees, hears and acts from love; that embodies the Christ Consciousness. Embodying the unitive state is a process.

Virtues: loving, beauty, kindness, protection, making, creativity, giving, nurturer, omniscient, all hearing, all seeing, just, aware, forgiving, generous, limitlessness, wisdom, powerful, first and last, manifest and hidden, majesty, honor, enriching, light, the guide, truth, calm, content, compassionate, courageous, determined, enthusiastic, faithful, flexible, free, gentle, healing, integrity, happy, honest, humility, magical, patient, positive, practical, resourceful, respectful, responsible, self-confident, sense of humor, sweet, tolerant, trusting, and others.
You could also call these harmonic qualities, qualities of the Light, of God. (There are also qualities of God that are seen as negative from the limited view, such as destroyer or avenger—but when held in the larger view, there must be breaking down to build something new, there must be cause and effect).

Vulnerable I & Vulnerable II:[201] Vulnerable I is that place where you feel—and believe—that you are weak. That is, you are "open" to attack, overwhelm, etc. Vulnerable II is the place that is an open and flowing system, with an undefended heart. This consciousness can get hurt, doesn't protect against it, learns from it and holds the incident with compassion. This is the state that lives fully, believes in it's own strength and love, and says "yes" to life/God.

---

201. This definition is from a brilliant colleague and therapist, Bill Colagrande, Phoenicia, NY.

Additional Materials

CHAKRA CONSCIOUSNESS

The chakras[202] are energy centers located at 7 areas of the body (some disciplines have more and some less). They are energy vortices that bring in life force to nourish the body. Each is connected to a gland.

The chakras regulate our energies and demonstrate by their shape and condition the state of that area of the body and all attendant organs, tissues and bones. The healthy shape of each chakra is like a cone. The second through the sixth chakras have cones in front and in back. The first and seventh have one cone. These cones spin clockwise, indicating a healthy chakra, and counterclockwise, indicating an unhealthy condition. Sometimes the cones are flopped over and the spin is uneven. Sometimes they are threadbare. Any impairment of the chakric cone indicates a problem with the area of the body the chakra "covers."

An understanding of the levels of consciousness of the chakras is extremely helpful in understanding your state of being and the path of consciousness. The shape, movement and condition of these vortices can be read by a clairvoyant and can be used to diagnose physical, psychological and emotional issues.

A critical mass of healing in the first three chakras (the incarnational chakras) form the chalice, which holds the spiritual chakras (states of consciousness) above. The healthy ego pursues and sustains the spiritual awakening. The positive will brings God through the material—which is, love applied through thought, emotion, will, physical expression.

---

202. There are many wonderful books on the chakras. A favorite of mine is: Judith, Anodea, *Wheels of Life—A User's Guide to the Chakra System,* 7th Printing (St. Paul, MN: Llewellyn Publications, 1990.

Our level of consciousness rises through the chakras through our effort at healing our blocks. What is at first achieved through striving can, at a certain point, happen without striving and becomes our ground of being.

The purified ego becomes the vehicle for love. That is, our alignment becomes deeper and stronger so that everything—the mind, emotions, the body—are in service to the heart.

First Chakra: The root chakra is located at the perineum. The gland is the adrenals. There is the wonderful metaphor of the snake for the healed energy of the first chakra. The snake slithers along looking for food. It keeps looking until it finds what it wants. It never doubts that the food is there to be found. It knows itself to be a part of the earth.

This level of our healing in the consciousness of this chakra is indicated by it's strength and sense of safety; the degree to which we trust that what we seek is there, and that we can get it. The healed consciousness of the first chakra does not expect to be an infant and have the world take care of us, but rather, if we do our part, the earth/life will be forthcoming.

The kundalini energy from our base (first) chakra vitalizes and energizes our body and energy field. It contains the primitive sex drive. As the being matures, the primitive sex drive of the first chakra, the sensuality of the second, and the love from the heart are united.

The existential wound of the first chakra is fear of death.

Second Chakra: The sacral center is located between the belly button and the pubic bone. The glands are the gonads. It is the chakra of the inner child, the consciousness of moving toward that which feels right/good and moving away from that which feels bad/wrong. It is the consciousness of connection and belonging, the tribal chakra. It is also the center of sensuality.

When wounded, it has unhealthy desires—addictions, and doesn't experience life fully. There is an inability to give and receive pleasure, or to play. There may be a pursuit of physical pleasure to an extreme.

We often close off to the feeling nature of the wounded inner child in the second chakra. We compensate and deny, and act out our defenses. When we have a certain amount of healing of the wounded child, we can open to the free, spontaneous and creative healthy child.

An open and flowing second chakra is the opening to sensing energies.

The existential wound of the second chakra is abandonment.

Third Chakra: The third chakra is at the solar plexis. The gland is the pancreas.

The third chakra is the culmination of the three incarnational chakras. The degree of ability to move about in the world successfully depends on the sum total of healing of the first three chakras.

It is the psycho/emotional "mind" of the 3-D. Power at this level is power over. The healthy third chakra has a sense of well-being, self acceptance, and an ability to act appropriately. The unhealthy third can be either bullying or collapsed, lacking in self-esteem or with an overblown sense of self.

As the healing of the incarnational chakras progresses, and the positive qualities of Truth and emotional healing are brought forth, the positive and harmonized ego actively seeks higher levels of consciousness. The more the "3-D mind" is witnessed and healed, the deeper purpose and connection to all things is revealed. The "little self" is given up, bit by bit, and the Real Self opens. The higher vibration becomes stronger and the guiding consciousness in life.

The existential wound of the third chakra is unworthiness.

Fourth Chakra: The fourth chakra is located at the heart. The gland is the thymus, sometimes called the "high heart." Its healed state is the consciousness of brotherhood that becomes unconditional love for all.

This is the "pivotal" chakra, that is, the one that is the determiner and leader of the rest, and the gateway through which the incarnational chakras can be healed, and the higher centers can unfold. My experience of the heart chakra is that it is very deep and vast. The outer layers carry the woundings of the heart: hurt; having our love rejected, which manifests as hatred—both inner and outer—separateness, and the choice not to love.

The inner heart carries the Divine spark, which we uncover through purification.

The feelings of the heart are necessary to the experience of the Divine.

Fifth Chakra: The fifth chakra is at the throat. The gland is the thyroid. This is the chakra of the unhealed ego dying into the surrender to God. It is speaking and listening, from wounding of these areas to hearing and speaking only love. It carries the ability to create positively or negatively. When healed, it carries the Word of Divine Truth, and can heal through sound vibration.

An open and healthy fifth chakra can hear our guides.

Sixth Chakra: The sixth chakra is located between the eyebrows. The gland is the pituitary, the "master gland." The sixth is the consciousness of inner looking and the third eye. The healthy sixth can discern light from dark, what is happening in Truth; and has deep powers of concentration. The wounded sixth can go into denial, have hazy thinking, manipulation using the mind, believing the fear of the unknown (death, unconscious, love, passing of time, our own darkness).

The third eye opens to see other dimensions.

Seventh Chakra: The crown chakra is our opening to the higher dimensions of spiritual energies. The gland is the pineal.

The wounding in this chakra is our misconceptions about the spiritual realms, fears of spiritual awakening, misunderstandings about God, trusting, and disconnection from the fundamental force of the universe. The healing of these misconceptions is a crucial level of healing which addresses our basic attitudes toward life and the workings of the universe. This level is often unconscious. We find our misconceptions with life/God by working with the disharmonies in our life.[203]

There is a Divine flow of energy that comes into the crown, our "daily bread," which we choose to use according to our evolvement.

---

203. See Format for Healing

This flow of Divine energy is like a central column that flows through the center of the chakras and out the base chakra into the heart of the earth. (I use this as a centering guide to stabilize my energies and to bring my intention to alignment with the highest I can reach).

The cones of the chakras at our backs are the will centers.

DIMENSIONS AND PLANES[204]

3rd Dimension—in this galaxy—4 planes
- First Plane: All Living People
- Second Plane: All other living things
- Third Plane (Astral) Ascended Masters: "un-ascended" spirits: Some living people who have a dual Existence. Ghosts.
- Fourth Plane: Inhabitants of the Hollow Earth

4th Dimension—in this galaxy—no planes
Location of the Souls of Mankind (ascended spirits of mankind) between Incarnations: devas: dark energies: auras become visible

5th Dimension (Universal)
4 planes, continuously linked with all planes in 3rd dimension, but only accessible by those who have the ability to do so.
- First Plane: Telephathic communications
- Second Plane: Dowsing, Shamanism and other altered States of consciousness
- Third Plane: Mediumship. Clairvoyance and other Metaphysical subjects
- Fourth Plane: All healing frequencies and vibrations

---

204. Dowsed by Geoff Stuttaford, Wise Man and Healer

6th Dimension

Creators, Nature Spirits, Gods (thought forms), other humans and humanoids On other planets, being known as "angels, including "guardian angels", "guides" and "helpers". Some of the latter are present in the 4th dimension to help ascended souls.

7th Dimension

There are no living things in this Dimension. It is the source of intuition and Creative ideas and is accessible by all living things in the universe.

8th Dimension

Contains the Universal Consciousness and the Basic Sources of good and evil.

Accessible only by those who are dedicated to the following either of the Paths.

These include such beings that are known as Archangels of Light and Darkness.

9th Dimension

The Great Spirit/Creator or equivalent

Note: When I asked about the various Gods and Goddesses who are worshipped on this planet, I was told that these were invented by mankind and exist only as thought forms. Any kind of prayer is equivalent to the intent used by dowsers and healers, and is a function of the sub-conscious mind.

ENERGETIC CLEARING AND PROTECTION:

.Every morning as you are waking and every evening as you are falling asleep, before and after you work with someone as a helper, clear your field, your room, your house, and the space above your house and into the ground below.

Method: Use your imagination to "see" a ball of white light about Three feet above your head (this is present as your 12th chakra). Direct that light to stream downward and wash through your body and your field carrying away any constriction/density with it. Then, visualize your aura egg, fill it with a clean, bright color (muddied colors contain densities); see the edge of your aura and imagine it being sealed. I imagine that an inch or so becomes very strong and impervious to every energy but love. Method: Imagine yourself surrounded with mirrors. Method: Hold your hands in front of your face, palms together, The tips of your fingers pointing in opposite directions, Pull your hands apart in opposite directions, then take your dominant hand and make an arc from the top of your spine down the front of your body to your base chakra. (This is very effective for clearing energetic cords*—you can also use your intention). Method for living space: Use your imagination to "see" a vortex of white light that whirls around your room carrying away any dense energy. Do this for your room, your house, the land surrounding, and above and below your house. You can also use Sage, Dragon's Blood, or just cover with rubbing alcohol 4 Tbsp. Epsom salts in a small frying pan and light to smoke 'um out. Especially with Dragon's Blood and Epsom salts, you will want to vacate the space for a while.

MANIFESTATIONS OF THE LOWER SELF ON THE DIFFERENT LEVELS OF CONSCIOUSNESS:[205]

"Unitive: The lower self is the dark side of God.
The lower self is God in the guise of forgetting itself.
The lower self is God in search of itself.
The lower self is God.

205. Thesenga, Susan, *The Undefended Self: Facing the Shadow…Freeing the Light… Becoming Whole* (Madison, VA: 1988) "What is the Lower Self?" p.155.

Transpersonal:

The lower self is our collective negative archetypes including the devouring mother, the castrating bitch, the bad witch, the temptress. And the archetypes of the savage father, the brutal husband, the black magician, the horned devil.

The lower self is all the devils and the demons who strive to tempt us toward power, separation and despair.

The lower self is our avoidance of pain, our refusal to hope, our commitment to separation.

Adult Ego Level:

The lower self is the egocentric adult, wanting to be "king/queen
Of the mountain," choosing control and sadism with other people,
And domination over the natural world, choosing power over love.

The lower self is the bitter and blaming adult, masochistic and dependent, identified with being the victim and punishing others with our own misery, unwilling to take responsibility for our lives.

The lower self is all the defenses we erect not to feel our self-responsibility and our vulnerable humanity, our shared brother and sisterhood with all other beings on the planet.

Child Level:

wounded, fearful, suspicious, unwilling to trust, egocentric child, selfish, greedy, willful. The lower self is the crust of defenses we erect in order not to feel the intense vulnerability, pain, and disappointment of childhood."

TRANSFERENCE/COUNTER-TRANSFERENCE

Transference and Counter-transference are *unconscious* mental/emotional/physical/ spiritual energy.

Transference is the pasting on (projection), of our unconscious, unresolved issues with God onto our parents. Then, we transfer our issues with our parents onto authority figures, our beloveds and others.

Our unresolved issues with God are those areas where we have forgotten certain aspects or qualities of the Divine, i.e., omnipresence (wound, abandonment), omnipotence (wound, helplessness), mercy (wound, abuse), etc. We have remembered many essence qualities of God, as evidenced by the areas of our life that are in harmony (healthy body, good food, family, a warm bed, beautiful possessions, friends, animals—a great many when we pay attention). To say it another way, we have some areas of our lives that are in harmony (where we have "remembered" God) and some that are in disharmony (where we have "forgotten" God).

The first level of transference with our parents comes from a split that is carried over from our previous lifetime. The influence of each parent and your attitude toward them, represents a two-fold split that you could not resolve before you entered this life. Our negative involvement with each parent represents two ways of reacting, two fundamental attitudes, that govern your unconscious automatic reactions to life situations. You react to life as you once reacted to your parents.

The second level of transference is the pasting on of our unresolved issues with our parents onto teachers, healers, leaders, and authority figures of all kinds, our beloveds and others. These issues with our parents come about because we have a "listening" to be wounded in those areas of "forgetting." The child feels the pain of the wound, the pain becomes too great, the event gets frozen in time and a defense is created to cover up and protect the wounds so that they are never felt again. The child associates feeling the pain again with dying.

The three primary defenses of aggression, submission and withdrawal all carry a negative stream. This negative stream carries a "no" to God, with a negative intent to destroy and a pleasure in the dark. These energies want to stay hidden, and are invested in the status quo.

A compulsion arises in the child to recreate the scene again and again; trying to get in the present what was needed in the past. The awareness of the energies of the wounding and defenses are pushed into our unconscious and influence our thoughts, emotions and actions. Since the awareness of these energies has dropped into the unconscious, we become aware of them indirectly through the disharmonies in our life. These disharmonies are the signals as to where to find our defense, our wound, and by being willing to see, feel and know *everything* about ourselves, we track back to the "teaching" (the essence quality of God that we are now ready to "remember" on mental, physical, emotional and spiritual levels). Our parents, therefore, give us the gift of catalyzing in us deep teachings. As we work through the wounding through our parents, we don't condone any negativity from them but rather let ourselves feel all our feelings, are willing to know the truth of what happened and know that they brought in what we needed most at this point in our path to God.

Working with the transference with our beloved is a deep walking with God. This person that we spend so much time with, that we commit to, that we "depend" on, soon becomes the recipient of our "paste-ons." If we are unconscious to our unresolved issues with our parents (stand-ins for God) the wounded child in us expects--demands!--to be treated in a certain way, to be agreed with, to be understood completely, to have our negativity accepted--never mentioned or confronted--and be loved anyway, to be given all that we did not get and are longing to get from our parents. We may even elicit from the other behavior that is not a predominant behavior pattern in them, because our energies are vibrating so strongly. Our energies are consistently bombarding the other with our demands, spoken or not spoken. We are manipulating by aggressing, withdrawing, or submitting to have it "our way." And, we are experiencing this from our beloved, as well. By holding our relationship as a relationship with the Divine, we can look at ourselves in truth, own our part in the disharmony, and fall deeper and deeper into unconditional love.

The following are some definitions[206] of Transference from the "therapy" model, and so are limited in their scope, but they may help the fullness of your understanding:

---

206. These definitions were included in a class handout and the Newsletter distributed by the Core Energetics Institute in New York City.

"*The person misunderstands the present in terms of the past; and then, instead of remembering the past, he strives without recognizing the nature of his action, to relive the past and to relive it more satisfactorily than he did in childhood. He "transfers" past attitudes to the present.*" *(Fenichel, 1915)*

"*An attempt to learn, by a series of rehearsals, how not to be helpless or powerless in a situation which originally found us so—the original situation being "remembered" although, not consciously recalled.*" *(Silverburg 1918)*

Reacting to somebody else as if they were a significant person from your past, such as your mother or father. The major dilemma that existed in the past is brought to the present situation. It says, "I will tell you who you are and I will deal with you in that way."

"*Transference comes up when our wounds are about to be exposed/ catalyzed.*"

Some relationships are based on transference: I will play this role for you, if you will play this role for me.

Transference is a vital tool for understanding the experience of the other.

Positive transference always leads to negative transference—because the person is asked to be someone they are not.

Transference is the sum total of the emotionally guided thoughts, feelings, physiologic reactions and anatomical posturings that the client initiates spontaneously and intuitively towards the therapist.

(PAMELA CHUBBUCK, CORE ENERGETIC INSTITUTE, 1991)

> *"I can get all bent out of shape trying to handle this stuff, unless
> I understand that transference is also a part of trying to get
> something right. I need to honor it and treat it as a song of
> change, a healing moment... As therapists, we too readily get
> caught up in the content of the transference, negating the in-
> tent...It is work with this intent that leads to healing."*

> (BARRY WALKER, CORE ENERGETIC NEWSLETTER, 1991)

Transference with leaders and authority figures:

The leader is seen either as the good parent (positive transference), or as the bad parent (negative transference). The positive transference can switch at any time to the negative. In positive transference, the teacher/healer will be put on a pedestal with an energy of pseudo-love, the sickly sweetness of the "good boy/girl. Often this person gives their power to the healer/teacher, looking for all the answers, wanting to be the child. In negative transference the leader becomes the parent who didn't satisfy the child's needs for safety, security, love, recognition, etc. There will be rage and revenge for not living up to expectations and unreasonable demands. The demand is for no disap-pointments, no pain, protection, the "parent" giving total fulfillment to the strong and unfillable needs, unconditional love no matter how much destructive acting out is done.

We unconsciously recreate the climate of our childhood while our conscious mind rationalizes our feelings, actions and the giving away of our power with distorted attitudes of "honoring," "surrendering," "harshly confronting for the sake of truth," etc.

The person in transference with a leader unconsciously wants their own personal, biased god. They want a "good" leader, one who indulges and is strong/powerful. They want someone to run their life, and at the same time carry resentment for it. There will be envy, and a reluctance to accept the responsibilities as well as the benefits of leadership.

In the transferencial situation the leader is not seen as a human being with gifts and faults, and someone who has a private life. They are seen as the satisfier of needs, the big "tit", so to speak. The leader is seen as a "source" for what the inner child wants, a need that can never be satisfied. Therefore, the "child" is angry with the leader and resentful. When the leader "makes a mistake" or is seen in any way as vulnerable, an energy called "kill the leader" can emerge. The leadership is criticized, an attempt made to discredit, or perhaps an old slight is brought up to make the leader bad and as a way of punishing and toppling them from their pedestal at a time when the leader appears to be weak. All attention and focus are on the faults/mistakes of the leader to hide the emotional reaction of the child. Or, the transference energies bring the person into the role of caretaker. An attempt may be made to infantalize the leader, with a pulling and/or control in the "giving".

A leader has to have a strong identification with their conscious ego self, a commitment to look for God's Truth, and be willing to "take" the energies. To hold a centered, loving, deep communion with God so that the wealth of information in the transference energies can be seen, understood and utilized to help the student in their path to oneness. The leader accepts the mantle of leadership with a willingness to contain all the energies, to stay pure and not take from the students (to be liked, loved, adored, made bigger than life, fawned over, etc). True leadership comes forth from the impulse to give unselfishly.

Counter-transference:

Counter-transference is the same as transference and is experienced in reciprocation to the energy of the "paste on" from the other. It is reacting from your own wound to someone making you who you are not. Ideally, the leader can contain their reactions, maintain the loving witness, and bring awareness to our own healing.

Finding Transference/Counter-transference:

The foundation: Know yourself—everything, from the highest and purest that your heart can reach, to the lowest, most selfish pocket of your unconscious. If you are aware of your defensive patterns, if you know your child well, and if you understand your male/female balance, you will have a strong clue as to the energies that will catalyze transference/counter-transference.

Bibliography

Bailey, Alice A., *Esoteric Healing, Volume IV, A Treatise on the Seven Rays*, 10th Printing, New York: Lucis Publishing Company, 1980.

Carey, Ken, *The Starseed Transmissions*, New York: HarperCollins Publishers, 1984.

Ferrini, Paul, *Love Without Conditions, Reflections of the Christ Mind*, USA, Heartways Press, 1994.

Gerber, Richard, M.D., *Vibrational Medicine, New Choices for Healing Ourselves*, New Mexico, Bear & Company, 1988.

Hall, Robert K., *Out of Nowhere, Poems from the Inward Journey*, California: Running Wolf Press, 2000.

Hawkins, David R., M.C., Ph.D, *Power vs Force, The Hidden Determinants of Human Behavior*, West Sedona, AZ: Veritas Publishing, 2002.

Hazelden Meditation Series, *Each Day a New Beginning*, Minnesota: Hazelden Educational Materials, 1982.

Judith, Anodea, *Wheels of Life, A User's Guide to the Chakra System*, Llewellyn Publications, 1990.

Ladinsky, Daniel, translated by, *Love Poems from God, Twelve Sacred Voices from the East and West*, New York: Penguin Group (USA), Inc., 2002.

Pathwork Lectures: Channeled Lectures, available at www.pathwork.org; or contact the New York Region Pathwork, 74 Main Street/Box 66, Phoenicia, NY 12464, 845-688-2211, www.pathworkny.org—Sevenoaks Pathwork, 403 Pathwork Way, Madison, VA 22727, www.pathworkmid-atlantic.org—Pathwork of California, 4716 32nd Street, San Diego, CA 92116, 800-779-2147, www.pathworkcalifornia.org (there are other centers as well)

Stone, Joshua David, Ph.D., *Soul Psychology, Keys to Ascension*, Sedona, AZ: Light Technology Publishing, 1994.

Thesenga, Susan, *The Undefended Self: Facing the Shadow…Freeing the Light…Becoming Whole*, Virginia, 1988.

Acknowledgements

I have received many beautiful teachings from teachers of different disciplines. The most pivotal to my personal process that I am aware of at this time are the following:

From the Pathwork, I learned to understand and face my darkness; from the Buddhists I learned to accept pain and embrace loving kindness; from the Sufi's I learned passion for God; from my Core Energetic Training (bodywork) I learned to allow and accept the spectrum of my feelings; from my energy teachers I learned to meet and explore the unseen worlds. From the teachings of Jesus I am learning to get practical with my Love.

From my inner guides, I have learned that there truly is deep love and help from the universe, and more, that it's a friendly universe.

From my sons, I learned about how powerful love can be, and how completely and naturally unconditional. They have been my inspiration at every level of my spiritual journey.

From my daughter-in-law, I learned how loving, inclusive and balanced a healthy ego could be.

From my grandchildren, I have learned that the heart is limitless.

From my dearest friend, Joan, I have found the love of a kindred soul, and the rare gift of being seen, heard and understood. And, perhaps even more wonderful, she gives acceptance even when there's no agreement.

From my dear friends Len and Noah, I have found true friendship and love with men. I will cherish them in my heart always.

From my dearest love, Don, I'm learning how to receive cherishing, understanding, and love from the finest man I have ever known. The miracle is not so much that he loves me, but how much I love him.

I can't imagine what more a person could have, but I have a sneaking suspicion that God will continue to test my capacity for joy.

Printed in the United States
103311LV00004B/337/P

9 781587 369902